DISAPPOINTED BY GOD

by

UEBERT SNR, ThD

Copyright © 2004 by Uebert Snr, ThD

Disappointed by God
by Uebert Snr Mudzanire, ThD

Printed in the United States of America

ISBN 1-594679-67-3

All rights reserved solely by the author. The author guarantees all contents (except where quoted) are original and do not infringe upon the legal rights of any other person or work. No part of this book may be reproduced in any form without the permission of the author. The views expressed in this book are not necessarily those of the publisher.

Unless otherwise indicated, Bible quotations are taken from the Authorized King James Version. Copyright © 1999 by Thomas Nelson, Inc.

www.xulonpress.com

DEDICATION

To all those in pain and all those in suffering and also to my brother Kenneth who might feel disappointed by God.

CONTENTS

PART ONE

PRELUDE TO THE PROBLEM OF PAIN 13
A must read!

CHAPTER ONE

DISAPPOINTED BY GOD 15
When God is silent 18
The problem of pain 20

CHAPTER TWO

WHERE WAS GOD WHEN MEPHIBOSHETH WAS SUFFERING 21
A veil of affliction 22
The hope of a new day 25
In the comfort of a monster 28
The unexpected moment 29
The great controversy 31
A free will analyzed 31
The glitz and the glamour of a gift 34

The power of dominion 38
A problem fixing to happen 39

CHAPTER THREE

OUTCH! THAT HURTS **43**
    The confusion 45
    Moving beyond pain 48
    The devil doesn't know squat! 53
    The thief of time 55
    God's modos operandi 56
    When God when? 58

CHAPTER FOUR

AWAKENING A SLEEPING GOD **61**
    The many faces of evil 63
    Hold on 65
    Behold 65
    God does not foresee, He sees 66
    The prison of the mind 66
    Modos operandi 69
    When revelation comes: shush! 71
    The greatness of timing 72
    The anointing 75
    The power of dreams 76
    Opportunity 77

CHAPTER FIVE

MEETING THE REAL YOU IN THE MIDST OF GOD'S SILENCE **79**
    The lack of identity 82
    The power of an anointed friend or father 83
    God's unconditional love: the irony 84

Rhema and logos 85
The great analogy 87
God never starts until it is too late! 90
The law of limitations 92

CHAPTER SIX

DISMOUNTING THE ROLLERCOASTER OF PAIN 95
A dose of pain analyzed 96
God has a way 99
The riddles of God 101
What to do when you don't know what to do 102
Lord will your demands stop? 103
The widow's domain 104
A delay is not a denial 106
How to know if prayers are delayed or refused?....106

CHAPTER SEVEN

THE STUPIDITY OF FAITH 109
The foolishness of faith 110
Getting to grips with stupidity 111
Stupidity observed 112
The intelligence within the stupidity 113
The stupidity of voting 114

CHAPTER EIGHT

DEFENDING YOURSELF: THE ARMOUR OF GOD 117
Why did Peter drown if he had the amour? 119
Calming the storms of life 121
The facts of war 123

CHAPTER NINE

ONE MORE DAY WITH THE TOADS 125
  The point of reason 127
  Not another night with the frogs 129

CHAPTER TEN

THE POWER OF WHAT YOU ALREADY POSSESS 131
  Propelled by a vision to get a breakthrough 134
  A paradigm shift observed 136
  The menu of a breakthrough 140
  Your problem will bow to God 141

CHAPTER ELEVEN

SOMETHING IS ABOUT TO HAPPEN 143
  The council of fools 144
  Hoodwinked 144
  What if I… 145
  Who can understand God? 146
  The fellowship and the pain 147
  Don't hate the Coach, hate the game 148
  It is my life anyway 149
  A fixed fight 154
  This Jesus! 155
  Using your favor to get a breakthrough 156
  Pain, man and God 157
  The storm is over 158
  Before the end of the storm 158
  Confessions, scriptures and hidden verses 163

**Acknowledgements and References 165-169

'Meanwhile, where is God? This is one of the most disquieting symptoms. When you are so happy that you have no sense of Him, if you turn to Him then with praise, you will be welcomed with open arms. But go to Him when your need is desperate, when all other help is vain and what do you find? A door slammed in your face, and a sound of bolting and double bolting on the inside. After that, silence. You may as well turn away.'

C.S. Lewis
A Grief Observed

PART ONE

PRELUDE TO THE PROBLEM OF PAIN

The story begins of a skeptic sitting beneath a mulberry tree, carrying a rather blasphemous monologue with God. His disappointment with God stemmed from a seemingly simple watermelon he had analyzed attached to its tiny sterm. He wondered and pondered at what to him represented the stupidity of God. His mind raced from critiquing to criticizing how an all powerful God would be this unreasonable to have a big tree producing small mulberries whilst a small plant carried big fruits like watermelons.

He fantasized being God for what seemed to be an eternity and then thought of how if he becomes God, will correct the absurdity of what he was seeing by putting small mulberry fruits on a small plant and big melons on a big tree at the magnitude of the mulberry tree he was sitting under. As he tried to arrange what he thought God in his entire splendor messed up, a mulberry fruit fell directly on his nose. The skeptic jerked "thank God it was not a watermelon!" the skeptic yelled.

It is not the pain that a sufferer hates the most but the meaninglessness of it, the scarcity of an antidote and the mere fact of why it exists. As an author I did not pen down my own thoughts on the problem of pain, neither did I hide my frustrations in overemphasized clichés nor the answers to the "why and how" of pain in piled syllables and vacant clichés. Instead I waited and waited until the words you are holding came to me, filled my innermost being and demanded to be written.

CHAPTER ONE

DISAPPOINTED BY GOD

Real life is like a poem recited by a dunderhead replete by absurd clichés foreshadowing nonentity. It is just but graffiti from a lunatic fringe swamped by soaring yesterdays, searing todays, incommode and twinge stalking the blind and dark impulses of our minds. But if all our prayers for luxuries, needs, destarata or compulsions were met by the "shalls" and the "wills" of all God's promises then we would be definitely taking multiple siestas down in the slope valleys of Venice beside the Sultan of Brunei's limousine, perhaps swallowing farinose puree consume, wetting our seldom but expensive appetite in non-alcoholic champagne with the pages of our Bibles ajar at Ecclesiastes 5 verse 18:

> "It is good and comely for a man to eat and
> to enjoy...all the days of his life..."

Mere fantasy!!

Emblazoned in the dark recesses of our fantasies are apparitions of a mute, a dead deity, a God long impotent and carefree. A pool of stilly aura surrounds, encompasses and transmogrifies authors on pain into parasites, maggots, viruses, arbiters sifting through the wit of humanity and at most grinds them into just trivia for the tram and bus ride home. Though I feel like a mere shabby curate who strayed by a ray of chance in an arena full of juntas, one thing is never a faux-pas: many authors on pain air flaccid antidotes which seldom relate to their suffering audience. It is by this and on these pages that I seek to justify the existence of this book.

Instead of me being a wild idealist, wide-eyed dreamer crawling beneath the opaque arteries of the woeful, or worse an incorrigible fantasist- I answered a call, awakened a gift to examine grief, pain and suffering on a profound but Biblical plane without clouding my audience with personal stories, legends or tales obtained from confused scholars, their so - called intellectual adherents, or a bountiful of crack heads who like to sound ridiculous. In most cases they air weight dictums that are repugnant to a sufferer's single iota of tangible hope to uphold the power and the clear will of God with regards to Him regulating calamities.

However, the ancient adage of pain's reality can not be swept away, neither by any author's little panache nor the sweet little clichés that cloud the receding unpaged portraits of shine. It must be understood in the very generic sense that when an author's biro stops rolling, the ink that drooled on the manuscript dries up and the sun peacefully hides itself deep in the rubbles of cosmic jungles, still questions remain unanswered: is God some kind of superhuman freak who sits and stares at us over a glass of holy wine and laugh at us uncontrollably as we try to concoct the pieces of life's diabolic puzzle?

Are human beings a measly cosmic joke driven by a carefree abstract entity bearing a confused wand with an incalculable devilish appetite for acute suffering, deep pain and threnodeody? If not why is then that when we are deep in the verge of making ends meet it seems God moves the ends?, when our miserable lives turn better, it seems God turns them bitter? Is God under a shemzzle of a million lethargic apprenticeships focused on doom? Is He a mere entity quardquantrillion miles away with a dire obsession with machoism, perhaps spotting a swastika on His left bicep? Is He a gross nuisance juggling humanity and too many a cares in far smaller hands than he need use? Does God draw a line to say "this is where you suffer"? Does God get too involved in the endeavors of solving the hunger in Africa and the moral decadence of the United Kingdom that he is caught unawares by the earthquakes of Iran and the hurricanes of America? Is He busy preparing the mansions of heaven that He Has ignored our world? I, like Epicurus have to ask "Is God willing to prevent evil but not able? Then He is not omnipotent. Is He able but not willing? Then He is malevolent. Is He able and willing? then whence cometh evil? Is He neither willing nor able? then why call Him God?"

Where is God when Africa is rotting? Where is He when the hungry children of Ethiopia live with poverty that seems to know the destination of their habitat? When they are under an oppression that knows the backing of brute force? Where is God when the world is groaning with pain? Where is God when the children of Peru strive on hard labour for an occasional meal? if it be fair to call it a meal. Where is God when America, Britain, Asia, Africa, the Middle East and the world as a whole are in present shambles? Why has terrorism, natural disasters, divorces, hunger, poverty, financial constraints, wars, death, diseases etc become the order of the day?

Where was God when all the recorded few and the unrecorded many were suffering in biblical times? Where? What of Christ taking three days to go to the funeral of his friend Lazarus? He even claimed Lazarus was asleep. Where is God when the civilized world groans in pain with the effects of terrorism?

An overdose of melancholy braces the unnumbered scripts of those deep in the endeavor of unmasking the problem of pain and the puzzle of suffering. In their immeasurable strength to analyze the riddles of this evil among humanity - they have inclined their critiquing and analytical dexterity on individuals who only suffered as a form of chastisement from God after committing sins. Some however focused on the stupidity of it all without giving answers or antidotes thereof.

I neither wish to be viewed a fit antagonist nor do I wish to be viewed a genius, but I am driven by emotion to lob the questions: where is God when either good or bad people suffer? where was God when Mephibosheth was hurting, crippled and broken? What about Joseph? He dreamt and his brothers sold him to passer-bys. He ran away from the snare of adultery and ended up in jail. In jail he interpreted the cup bearer's dreams but after the fruition of the dream the cup bearer forgot about Joseph.

I can understand it when God punishes sin but where was God when an innocent and sinless five year old Mephibosheth was suffering? Why did Christ heal only one cripple at the pool of Bethsaida? Where was He when the cripple was suffering for thirty-eight years? Why did He ignore the others? Why does He allow suffering anyway? Any kind of suffering that is -why? Why? Why?

WHEN GOD IS SILENT

Many a time God's silence becomes more threatening than the catastrophe. It produces pockets of pain in our bosoms, derelicts the hope of a day, closes the door of opportunity and becomes larger than we can hardly comprehend. Day and year melt away in the cavernous gloom of our suffering life as we start carousing in amplified and ungoverned revelry. God's silence marks our lives with adverse, emergence circumstances, crisis, a time of real battle and real action. We become buffeted by pain and suffering that death as undesirable as it is opens its mouth to our dire admiration but where is this God? How can we locate him? Was God always like this?

To solve this riddle it must ring in our minds that there is nothing like spying to feed the meddlesome mind and sooth the scars of the heart.

May I be excused to move behind the prophet Isaiah as he removes all his clothes to preach naked to the people for three solid years at the command of a loving God. What about David who ripped the jaws of a lion, tore the bear to pieces only to be found later in-between the legs of another man's wife; Bathsheba, lead me to Elijah who by the Lord called fire to come down from heaven but in half of no time running for his life away from Jezebel - a woman sent to destroy God's work.

Show me Jacob a proven spiritual giant who danced all day long on his wedding day, only to be given a droopy eyed Leah in marriage instead of Rachel the apple of his eye whom he had worked for, seven years. When God is silent our lives delve into a bowl of amputated goals ushering Chicago elves, though mystified by abundant glory. Again show me Hosea as he closes his door to go forth and take a prostitute for a wife at the command of a loving God and I will show you Simon the separable who sank at the sight of the wind and nearly passed out when he mistook the Lord Jesus for a ghost.

He is the same Simon who rose from Simon meaning weak to Peter meaning the rock and to the devil in the space of just six verses, all because he had rebuked our Lord Jesus Christ from going through suffering [Matt 16 vs. 18-23]

As if that is not enough: I will show you many of Jesus' disciples who got killed for the gospel's sake. You might be compelled to question what happened to the almightiness of our loving God.

THE PROBLEM OF PAIN

Tantamount an opera, we dance to the heave of a diabolic, controlling maestro's baton. Death, sickness, troubled marriages, financial constrains, war, hunger, loneliness, natural disasters, stress etc drag us hither and thither in between the horns of a dilemma and ushers us in to the depth of life's suffering pages. Hell and the prowler object us to the proximity of a throng of hutched doppelganger demons that salivate, spit luminous and orbital flames.

How can we surmount this evil among us? What is really in this pain? What can be its purpose? What is really in it that even our Lord Jesus Christ (God in flesh) called Peter (the rock); Satan, when he rebuked Him from going through suffering. He even opened the door of auspicious discretion, subverted it, contra bounded it from His mind and opened His mouth to lecture His disciples including Peter on how best to suffer:

> "...ye shall weep and lament...ye shall be sorrowful...In this world ye shall have trouble..." [John 16 vs. 20, 33]

CHAPTER TWO

WHERE WAS GOD WHEN MEPHIBOSHETH WAS SUFFERING?

"Mephibosheth was five years old...and his nurse took him up and fled: and it came to pass as she made haste to flee, that he fell and became lame..." [2 Samuel4 vs.4]

Like any sufferer, Mephibosheth is neither legitimately authenticated nor accepted within the confines of the social, spiritual or political system he aspires. He is engrossed in a dim zone of an Eldorado, attempting to unmask the pangs of adversity and unplug the black codes of pain's serfdom. An oblique atmosphere giggles at him with crocodile teeth.

Mephibosheth is not a harlequin, just the devil's object of effort, a "sunshine" turned to night, a minute turned to hours, a reality turned to a wish and a day transformed into a decade. What hovers around the prologue of his life is the devil's junta of impalpable stratagems. The prologue emerges epilogue like. Hope has vanished, his family is massacred by a ruthless pagan army, he is crippled forever and his hopes for the kingly robes are robed within the party lines of an adversity that he neither orchestrated nor saw coming. No one will ever know his pain; he is just the product of a carefree nurse pressured by circumstances into a haste to flee.

> "...and it came to pass as she made haste to flee that he (Mephibosheth) fell and he became lame... [2 Samuel 4 vs. 4]

Imagine him as he tries to jerk an occasional smile, he is still but in a rush, down a tense jungle invented by a world that derelicts a couple sorrows of yesterdays and yesteryears and then surrogates them with a quard-quintrillion more. Can Mephibosheth pull a smile within a billion tears? Can he, through all the volumes of anguish consecrate himself anew to a silent world of a silent God?

To miss the melancholy of this young, feeble, mucus drooling and helpless lad is to miss every sense of the subject of pain. Mephibosheth as a sufferer has become two legs short of a palace, a pie short of a picnic and a candle short of a menorah. He is trapped within a world he never knew, wanted or wished. The hopes of a king in him are shattered, marred by an army of uncircumcised Philistines who destroyed his heirloom along with the people who offered him protection, let alone love. As for God, he is silent. He has become a mere abstract entity "quadquintrillion" miles away, untouchable, unmovable, rigid and invisible. God is just not in the vicinity even for a lame five year old. Oh my!

A VEIL OF AFFLICTION

Mephibosheth's heart cries "encore" for those bedtime stories of mythical princes, princesses, war captains and gothic kingly robes that filled the then unsheltered visage of his ears. His tears though flowing can never drown the pain

Disappointed by God

and suffering he is going through. His hopes have all crumpled without a trace. All are now cramped and held within the part lines of adversity and the lame legs, but what happens if God is going to forget Mephibosheth? Where will he find solace and more importantly where is this loving God? What if God is not interested in Mephibosheth's pain? Can God be accountable for the actions of the Philistines who killed his family, the nurse's uncalculated haste to flee and the choices of his family?

The ultimate episode of Mephibosheth's austere life exhibits the sheer reality of a doleful gong that had lingered in his mind from the tender age of five to the then Mephibosheth who now has a kid of his own. Nostalgia proliferated from memoirs of a palace life cut short preyed on him but didn't God say "let the little children come to me for the Kingdom of God is for such as these"? If this is the case, then where was God when Mephibosheth was hurting and suffering? Mephibosheth is in melee; he exposes the very depleting self esteem of an ex-prince caught up in a globe gone wild and a world gone bezzack. He opens his mouth to speak and utters the words:

"…such a dead dog as I am…"

Delays and obstacles are strewn along a sufferer's byways and highways in their boundless endeavor to regroup the valuable hinges of pain's invisible doorways. Like all pained people, Mephibosheth's life speeds towards twilight yet David, the one who took his throne, faces the dawning of a new day. All around Mephibosheth's paralyzed frame and his smelling habitat; unstoppable angelic plastered lips latently shower him with breakthroughs. Why are his prayers not answered? Why? Why? Why? Only his are not answered. Oh my!

Mephibosheth cannot endure the torture of a lingering,

ringing, consumptive and string attached latent and diabolic passion of the adversary but can he wait upon God's rhema and see beyond his disability for a moment? We all face it, this moment is not alien to any suffering person, it is a common texture of the rollercoaster of pain and suffering. We all are faced by its shackles. We are all in serfdom to its manacles and booths. When we are in pain we are open and are usually clouded by testimonies of other people we really were better at in our prayer life. Instead of critiquing we criticize. Instead of getting better we become bitter. We seem not to noticeably unmask and understand the reasons why God blesses others yet omits us.

In all that Mephibosheth does there is a patent toting up to the pain of Mephibosheth and a dirge of undeniable irony, the house he is in is **Machir's**, the name *'Machir'* itself means a *sell out* or that which is bought. Mephibosheth's name also has a meaning steaming with bleakness for it is rightly translated as *'from the mouth of shame'*. The town Mephibosheth is dwelling in is also short of hope for it is known by the name *Lode bar* which means *'no pasture'*. It is in itself situate of no hope, no fertility and no life. It has absolutely nothing except a silent God and a lame five year old under a sell out's roof. Oh! God!

Mephibosheth's anguish is seemingly chronic. It breeds a level of demise that God himself can not do any thing about for it is a product of fear which God in His sovereignty does not author and will never instigate. Its nature begets and weaves an attitude of surrendering to suffering and that impending desire to put God on the firing row: he is not alone in this block, even the prophet Isaiah who once preached naked for three years at the command of God- had this to ask:

> "Oh lord…wilt thou hold thy peace and afflict us very sore? [Isaiah 64 vs. 12]

Solomon, the philosopher, the one who commanded a great deal of intelligence and wisdom was baffled by pain on earth that he was forced by emotion to utter the most unexpected words ever heard from a giant in the faith.

> "Vanity, of vanities...all is vanity. What profiteth a man of all his labor under the sun...For all are sorrows and all his travail grief; yea, his heart taketh not rest in the night. This is also vanity. I have seen the grief which God has given...man..."

Jeremiah also lamented to God by proclaiming one of the worst things to say, let alone be found in the scripture (yet it is there because the Bible is God's truth and deals with truth of the happenings not cover ups) in Jeremiah 20 vs. 7:

> "Oh Lord thou deceived me and I was deceived"

THE HOPE OF A NEW DAY

The hope of a new day always groans paralyzed and motionless to every sufferer facing a possible breakthrough. Weary crimson tears of betrayal flow down those chapped and protruding chick bones. Mephibosheth's nights are all lit up by hades' electric fluorescents and the man in him lacks any trace of the expected positive optimism. In his mind is a resident spirit of defeat, something a sufferer usually abhors but absolutely should not have. He cannot lay down himself to bed. All is not well. Dreams for him never come easy; when they do they are just a pile of haunting graffiti in the brain of the ex-royal's feeble frame.

Years crept beneath the legs of Mephibosheth. Scars show. He now has a child of his own. He is now grown up, not in the mind but in the body and as for God, He is nowhere to be found. If he is nigh, then Mephibosheth can not see him. One can imagine the pain he is going through. He was supposed to be a king but then the Pharisees and the nurse diluted the reality of his supposed destiny. The people he loved most are extinct as are the hopes of a breakthrough and everything will remain ineffectual if every aspect of his life remains as it is, but if God heaves a fit of benevolence then what? And if He does not, then why?

To the nurse, the problem was as a result of the uncircumcised Philistines. To Mephibosheth everyone and maybe if not certainly, including God is blame worth. That sweetness of the once sweet little prince ebbed and died, not an echo was left. Still crumbed in the shadows of death, a glazed terror is frozen in Mephibosheth's suffering. He has been transformed into a traveler between vain love and an excruciating life but where is God? How can He stand aside whilst this prince turned orphan is suffering? A sandpaper teardrop squeezed its way against Mephibosheth's chapped skin. He jerks into a grimace, another day has passed and another is dawning. Now and maybe only now can he stand among the unstoppable lips that once blar-blar and blar-r-d around the disability of his inability, full of testimonies.

Pain is not Mephibosheth's problem or a sufferer's riddle but a symptom is. The problematic thing is our procrastination in surmounting these symptoms and our misunderstanding of how the devil uses a symptom. This misunderstanding is tantamount a pain killer for it cools down the pain but does nothing towards the eradication of the real problem which is the disease. Scars still show, wounds will still be there though the pain and suffering seem to have gone for a moment.

Pain and suffering can be promptly seized but the devil utilizes the symptom by getting you to believe that you were never delivered from the former at first, this happens long after the actual disease or suffering is terminated by God.

Disappointed by God

We are bombarded by the devil using symptoms to get us to believing that we are still under the serfdom of pain and suffering. After getting our breakthrough we should also know how to keep it by ignoring the adversary who is always using a symptom to get us to doubt the great work Christ performed in us. Maybe our major hindrance in surmounting either suffering or the symptom thereof is the church's obsession with the *spectacular* rather *than the supernatural* where the breakthrough really exists. The spectacular resides in the natural where pain also takes camp and the supernatural exists in the spiritual where the breakthrough has already been authored.

Pain and suffering are the most helpful agencies in a believer because they take you on a journey to realize what the state of your body is at any given time. Though Mephibosheth is in a very bad state of mind at least he understands humbleness and honour through pain hence the words 'such a dead dog as I am' Without these two we will die without knowledge but when we get hold of the purpose of pain and suffering we are ushered in to a place where we can prevent a catastrophe before hand. Mephibosheth's problem is to understand his perceived level yet failing to do anything about it. This is what I as an author have labeled the disease of *mal-realization*.

The realization of pain is not a limitation of humanity but a freedom to deeper understanding of our symptom. A breakthrough will truly come to you as a result of your apprehension of the magnitude of the pain you as a person are experiencing. This realization enlarges your very capacity to receive and embody a breakthrough. *You can not receive what you can not embody.* Mephibosheth tried it and it did not work. It should be noted without fail that if Mephibosheth remains drowned in his mental state of a dead dog and fail to enlarge his capacity to receive by his failure to take note of his symptom he will not receive anything from God unless God Himself shifts in His domain and pulls a fit of His benevolence.

It should be understood that there can never be joy where there is no pain; otherwise that which we will regard as 'joy' ultimately becomes suffering and pain. This is because joy is viewed using an eye that has seen the opposite of joy or mainly obtained from surmounted pain. Even the eternality of heaven is validated by the temporality of this earth. Again we can only understand the *greatness of a resurrection by recognizing the existence of death.* Pain is no different; to get a Mephibosheth with a breakthrough there should be a Mephibosheth who has suffered.

IN THE COMFORT OF A MONSTER

Sometimes we as sufferers are too comfortable within the serfdom of pain that we think of surmounting the obstacles in our conduit as a definite impossibility and a conundrum none can triumph over. Though we might not view it possible to have this shallow state of mind there is in our sub conscience, that degree of thought which dictates to us that 'we are deeply in pain and immersed in suffering that death is the only way out' but that sense is intensely rooted in the pits of hell. Somewhere in this world God expects us to be pain's voice of reason. David says of God 'You have exalted your name above all names'.

The revelation given to David is not a mere inkling of a desperate man trying to pile up syllables in his praises for his God but rather a clear indication of inspiration and revelation that every sober, mad, rich, happy, blessed or suffering individual should feed down their inner being and thrust up into their mind. The names that God is saying are under His own name comprise of everything in this universe for all things have names. We might not know of these names but the truth is open, everything including all our circumstances possesses a name.

If your cancer has a name do not be comfortable in it but tell your cancer God's name is above that disease and do not lose heart because *though you have the cancer, the cancer does not have you.* It is the same with every condition, be it pain or suffering. If you have a financial crisis then God's name is above that financial crisis. If your loved one is making the final gasps, bed ridden in a certain hospital somewhere tell that disease you have a God with a name above that disease. If you are in pain and suffering due to the circumstances around you then tell your circumstances that a great God with a name above them is coming. If your marriage is falling apart, please! talk to your marriage problem and tell it about the name of God, it will bow to it. Everything will bow to Jesus' name, come what may!

It is now time not to tell God about your problem but a time to tell your predicament whatever it is, about your God. Introduce your pain and suffering to your God and if your God is the great Jehovah it will without fail run away from you for His name is exceedingly greater than anything seen or unseen. Do not highly esteem the effects of your circumstance for by so doing you undermine the greatness of a God with a name that is above all names. Instead of comparing your circumstances to your ability to handle them you are spiritually and physically called to compare your circumstance to the *incomparable* magnitude of Jehovah's name.

THE UNEXPECTED MOMENT

Like any sufferer there is a time, Mephibosheth knew not when, a point he knew not where, a catastrophe he knew not which, a palace he knew not where; that marked a triumph from ragamuffin back into the scent filled kingly robes and the perks thereof. The void elements of his pained life have been waiting to be addressed yet God was silently rearranging the fallen pieces of his suffering life. God has made Mephibosheth elude the rhythm of his inner thoughts.

He removes him from an immense raging horror, a thunder of abuse and a life of lack. First there is a lucid gasp of zeal but it chokes yet nigh, soothing the dabs of notes within him. It is about time God! But this is only as an act of benevolence not something God is obliged to do or something Mephibosheth schemed.

> "And David said, is there yet any that is left of the house of Saul, that I may shew him kindness for Jonathan's sake?..that I may shew the kindness of God unto him. And Zibba said unto the king, Jonathan hath yet a son which is lame on his feet...then King David sent and fetched him... [2 Samuel 9 vs. 1, 3]

The exclamation that Mephibosheth makes is a patent indication of what all sufferers experience but then become too afraid of confronting God with. Mephibosheth as a real life story is a thorn in the flesh of many Christian apologetics authors. His state of mind can not grant Mephibosheth a ticket in to the breakthrough island. The story itself by offering Mephibosheth a new day seems to lack the existence of a direct answer to pain or the exceptional antidote to suffering, yet in all its seemingly failure to unplug the steps to follow when under pain and suffering the book itself managed without a shadow of doubt to introduce to us a merciful God.

However, even if Mephibosheth has found favor in the new King, David; one thing is not settled. David is now King. Let us face it this is not to be thus for this is supposed to be Mephibosheth's place not David's.

THE GREAT CONTROVERSY

"And David said unto him (Mephibosheth) fear not: for I will surely shew thee kindness for Jonathan thy father's sake.....And he (Mephibosheth) bowed himself, and said what is thy servant... [2 Sam 9 vs. 7-8]

Though these words are carefully woven in David's mouth there is laid an exigency and a dire need as it were to remind him that this kingship really belongs to Mephibosheth. The crown that now adorns his head, the perfumes, the kingly robes and the kingdom perquisites are if you come to your senses, Mephibosheth's. It might seem sensible and divine to think of David as the rightly appointed king but the fact is Mephibosheth is supposed to be the real king PERIOD. This will conversely acquire no upshot if we take a moment in time to scrutinize one of God's gifts to men, *free will*.

A FREE WILL ANALYSED

In Genesis 1 vs. 26 the creator establishes a decree that deposits precincts to His operations on earth and that grants the endowment of freedom of choice to the creature. In it lies the blue print of God's own word being an edict unto Himself also, by this God is forced by the decree He Himself authored not to break His own word for He says in another scripture 'my word will not return to me void' Imbedded in the verse (Genesis 1 vs. 26) are four words of immense significance '...let them (you and I) have dominion...' By these words, according to the inspirational bowl in me and also to the revelation received by the man of God Dr Myles Munroe, God was distancing himself from ruling the earth, instead he bestowed the dominion to his creature with a humus body (A spirit in a dirt suit) David concurs:

'you (God) have given man you have created to be ruler of the works of your own hand'

In essence this weaves the inescapable reality that an Almighty and loving God's degree of affection for his creatures made you and I the ruler of this world, *not Him*. Taking this into proportion every human bad or right has the freedom of choice, the right to choose peace, the right to destroy, the right to hate and the right to love, all because of this freedom of choice. Abraham was a pagan when God first spoke to him. He was a pagan with the right to choose and as a human he had been endowed with the dominion over everything surrounding him including the unsearchable right to choose bad or right. If God had not given Abraham or us this will to choose then God Himself would become an *abstract remote control*, a control freak entity and us robotic structures dancing to the heave of his mighty, uncompromising, irrevocable and unseen hand. But God being God has provided you and me with something called prayer so as to communicate with Him.

Dr Myles Munroe vividly delineates prayer as an earthly license for heavenly interference. By this he means prayer is giving God dominion and right to interfere in the affairs of men where they have failed to reach as mortals. We all should understand that the earth has been granted to us, we have the license over everything on earth so for God to help us with our problems there is need for a transfer of the license and this is done through prayer. God Himself has to obtain the license to interfere with our affairs, from us and from no one else (even for an act of benevolence which is studied is due to the intercessory prayers). So Mephibosheth's problems came as a result of the freedom of choice that Saul his grandfather had, his nurse had and the Philistines who killed his family had and not as a result of the will of God. We all have choices, Adam had a choice which ushered us all in to the chains of suffering and pain's serfdom, so did Eve.

It can be viewed beyond reasonable doubt that God was not the one who fashioned the bayonets of the Philistines, sharpened their swords, gave speed to their horses, drove the horses of Jonathan and Saul his father but these were created and formed by the involved parties' own will to resolve national differences through the agent of war. God was not chairing their war table. Mephibosheth consequently can neither censure God for the actions of his family nor for the blood thirst feats of the Philistine army; he can only plead for God's mercy upon his life, nothing more. Free will causes the best if we adhere to the creator who purposed it and might create the worst in us if we can not be vigilant enough to view its boundaries. We cause evil and not God for *evil is a privation* and not a thing that it can be created.

It is not about God's fault but all is about us failing to use for good the saccharine freedom we were given, but us being born of spirit we are transformed into spirits. We become *spiritual bodies having a natural experience* and it is in this natural realm that pain resides and we like Mephibosheth are not exempt. Though the Bible decrees that God loved us before we loved him we as human beings have a God given strong mandate and a divinely authored free will that dictates to us that we are the ones who initiate the level and strength of intimacy with God and not vice versa hence the scripture:

> "Draw nigh to God and He will draw nigh to you"

My Bible says everything is born after its own kind so if we are all born of a God who is powerful, then we can overcome our predicaments indefinitely. Mephibosheth is not aware of the level he is supposed to be a feature of; by so doing he groans in ponds of ignorancia-factata and wells of heartrending gooey. Unlike Mephibosheth's inability to settle within the word of God and the incapacity to seize being subdued by his circumstances, we can prevail in the midst of the highest catastrophe of our pains and sufferings if we get to comprehend God the way He desires us to understand Him and rate highly our stratification in the Lord. With this in mind and in our Christ occupant hearts rooted in our bosom from the foundation of the world, pain becomes a *gift the church forgot*! A side effect of the free will we can not escape until we give up the right to choose and a regulator of our very inner beings.

One of the greatest writers to ever come out of the United Kingdom realized the riddle and penned down without hesitation his observations;

> Perhaps we do not realize the problem so to call it enabling finite free wills to co-exist with Omnipotence it seems to involve at every moment almost a sort of "Divine abdication."
>
> C.S. Lewis

THE GLITZ AND GLAMOUR OF A GIFT

It is the seemingly senselessness of pain being a gift that burns more than pain itself. The scarcity of the ability to discern the power of a gift within this usually unclaimed gift of pain pulls no punches and decants an ocean of poignant juice over every sufferer and over the sizzling slates of a pained mind. Mephibosheth also could not realize it. He ran away from its absoluteness and lounged on a pillar of no anticipation. It is at this echelon of the glamour and the glitz that few pained people recess in deep acceptance and reverence to the presence of 'class' within the ostensibly atrocious gift of pain.

A lack of revelation and inspiration pertaining to the 'gift the church forgot' cripples, nullifies and transforms the body of Christ into a feeble skeptic filled, senseless, archaic and powerless and puts it right at par with a gathering of certified dunderheads and mentally deprived saints and 'aints' who are simply believing as a *matter of duty* and nothing else. We have run amok with the gospel of pain that the body of Christ has now brewed a different perception and gist to this so called monster among us. But what glamour can be found in pain anyway that the church and the body of Christ must teach it or rather promote it?

Firstly, a gift is always a mystery webbed in the manifestation of both the blessing and the catastrophe. It is a package God gives at the altitude of what He understands and what He knows past reasonable doubt that those with the mind of Christ will get to grips with. The blessing manifests itself in deeds both spiritual and physical. Mephibosheth's manifested through lame legs and a slaughtered family. It might seem rebuff gazing at the gift within these catastrophes by only basing a ridiculous squabble on the tangible pain that he is going through both physically and emotionally but the very catastrophe confirms the gift. God says the gift of a man maketh a way for him so without looking at the pain of Mephibosheth let us wait until we discover where he moves to from now on so as to really establish if there is a way made for him by him being lame. If there is, then even without a revelation (though this is a revelation) you can infer he has a gift.

It is a sure sign that when God anoints you He anoints in secret yet the manifestation is shown openly .The devil is caught up unawares then he tries to counter attack by destroying yet God with his goodness proves to the devil that he will always have limitations with reference to the anointed and the not so anointed few. In fact God does not react, he acts. Though the devil infuses a mistaken view of himself being above and ahead of every situation the truth can not be hidden, he is always trailing behind. The devil is always befuddled at how God turns pain and suffering into clear gifts that in turn become great elements of faith to the ones in the serfdom of suffering and the ones in pain.

God wakes up the gift that lies dormant in us usually through pain and suffering. Mephibosheth was a comforter of David and more importantly a kingdom stamp to show how merciful David was by remembering his friend and "brother" Jonathan. It is in this gift that David enlarged his name at the same time enlarging God's glory. It seems to me as an author that where David thought he was gaining ground by works of charity he was unaware that God had ordained Mephibosheth to be thus and also that God was getting glory through all this. Note: He did not cause Mephibosheth's suffering but he employs his pain as a lesson to him, as David's stamp of loyalty, as a glory magnetizer and a strong reminder to the body of Christ.

DIVERSITIES OF GIFTS AND CALLINGS

There are diversities of gifts and callings that Christ's people like you and I have to get acquainted with before we blame and accuse God of something we ourselves could not make head or tail of. Gifts differ at the discretion of the Spirit and pain is a gift that is not created but only allowed. To Elizabeth God assigned the birth of John the Baptist and he confirmed that among all born of women there was no greater person than John. The same 'John the Baptist' is given a commission to forerun the coming of the Lord. All seem to be desirable gifts until John is killed at the hand of the devil, with the allowance of God and Elizabeth is forced to bury her gift (John).

Elijah is given prophecy as an office and Namaan is offered power like none other as a captain of the Syrian Army, but with prophets usually facing death from the likes of Namaan many would have chosen Namaan's power and profession for a gift but then God allows leprosy to afflict

Namaan. Elijah who has a risky (I Kings 19 vs. 4) occupation has the ability to be Yahweh's point of contact in the healing of Namaan's leprosy and the exhortation of the whole land of Israel.

Mary has the gift of giving birth to the Lord Jesus Christ and to the crippled at the pool of Bethsaida is allowed (note the word allowed) thirty-eight years of missed opportunities all for the glory of God.

All these gifts have a down side to them but the most interesting aspect of all of their differences is that they are a sign to us about what God in his understanding glory feels and knows without a shadow of turning what their roles in our lives are. To God the word gift is always something that pushes us closer to him than we are at any present moment, yet to us a gift remains something that we believe is to be enjoyed and appreciated by our senses irregardless of what its giver assumes or feels about it. To our carnal minds this does not have to do with what God feels, understands, knows or thinks but in what we as people are comfortable with, at home with and really in love with. That is conversely a grave miscalculation and a gross error in the mathematical center of our aspiring divine minds and a bad cell in what should be a guileless body of Christ.

Let us understand God's views on every subject of our lives for it is in this stance that we as mortals have to find a divine sense of proportion by understanding the word gift using God's own definition and not our own carnal understanding of the word. It is not all about us but all is about God so every time we get locked within the part lines of adversity let us look and see if our pain and suffering phases do not have heaven's blue print. If they have then consider, and when your nights turn to a morning then rejoice. It is not because God causes evil to happen to his children but without escaping it he will have allowed it but all for the good purpose. Paul concurs

"Every thing works together for good for those who love God"

Your ability to understand the principles God employs to enlighten you about the glamour and the glitz of pain will forever augment your capacity to receive a breakthrough. No one can receive what they can not embody and there are in life states of the mind, battles and conditions we have to wrestle with in our understating of pain so as to increase this capacity to embody a breakthrough. We have to disembark without waiting and without failing from the Mephibosheth state of mind that says "Such a dead dog as I am…" and have dominion over the situation and tune into the frequency of our creator who endowed his creatures with the profound gift of dominion and the unmerited free will. We are neither dogs nor servants but 'to them that believed gave He the rights to become children of God'.

THE POWER OF DOMINION

Having dominion does by no means make you a dominator but a commander. A dominator always breeds a dictator and a dictator does not operate within the boundaries of rules set by God but operates within the circumference of their own rules which are bent and twisted to accommodate their lusts. (*If you speak 'English' you might see me as being flawed concerning these words but if you speak 'Tongues' you will see the sense*). It is a great mind that understands it will not take financial muscles to have dominion for even Mephibosheth in his poverty and in the ugly shadows of his defeated mind had a lot he dominated including his thought life, hence he could not get out of his problem but remained lamenting: "such a dead dog as I am". A God inhabitant commander operates within the set rules and will by no means go out of bounds or think less of his post unless the rules dictate so. He keeps his thoughts captive to Christ.

God in the book of Genesis did not make us dominators but He placed us in, and granted us dominion to rule over all of our circumstances that is why the Bible proclaims

"Concerning the work of my hands command ye me…"

In order to fit into God's plan for your life you have to first be a misfit like Mephibosheth, otherwise you will never know where you really fit because a search for where to fit is as a result of failing to fit somewhere. When a deep calls to a deep then there is a deep to respond to the call otherwise the deep should not call at all. So to find the right place and hinge to fit in, you have to initially look and find where you do not fit and pain is the catalyst to this entire journey. Remember for any mortal to understand what a straight line is, they have to be first acquainted with a crooked one. By so saying you like Mephibosheth might be in pain as a point to starting your journey towards a godly place were you fit without a shadow of turning and where you hap into a journey haul-aging you from glory to glory and sitting you from blessing to blessing.

But what will we do then if we face a problem we can not stop? If we have reached a point we can not control with what we believe is endowed in us? e.g. death.

A PROBLEM FIXING TO HAPPEN

Another story begins as told by Jeffrey Archer and reported from the mouth of DEATH herself:

There was a merchant in Baghdad who sent his servant to the market to buy provisions and in a little while the servant came back, white and trembling, and said, Master just now when I was in the market-place I was jostled by a woman in the crowd and when I turned I saw it was Death that jostled me.

She looked at me and made a threatening gesture; now lend me your horse, and I will ride away from this city and avoid my fate. I will go to Samarra and there death will not find me. The merchant lent him his horse, and the servant mounted it, and he dug his spurs in its flanks and as fast as the horse could gallop he went. Then the merchant went down to the market-place and he saw me standing in the crowd and he came to me and said why did you make a threatening gesture to my servant when you saw him this morning?

That was not a threatening gesture, I said, it was only a start of a surprise. I was astonished to see him in Baghdad, for I had an appointment with him tonight in "Samarra.

The reality of what we can not change in the natural is a mere illusion, a mere shadow of the nonexistent things, it is not even a reflection of the spiritual realm but there exists three levels of response to the subject of pain and the things within it we can not seem to alter, one is to disintegrate- get angry about your situation, get ugly about it and do nothing, the other is to implode- blame yourself and those around you about it and again absolutely do nothing, the final is to swim with the tide- accept what God can only change or alter, rebuild your prayer altars and ask God to fight your wars for you. Remember though you have dominion you are only the body of Christ and the head remains Christ Jesus and just as the Head can not do anything without the body so the body can not do anything without Jesus Christ its Head.

Some things in life can not be out done or prevented no matter how we might try. Paul's shadow healed many people, he even healed people using handkerchiefs as a point of contact but you find him writing a letter to Timothy instructing him to drink a little wine as medicine. Why did he not send Timothy one of his anointed aprons? You might ask what became of his healing ministry but the truth is; only God knows why it was so BUT the greatest mistake is to assume that your situation is one of the few that can not be altered. Every time we get at loggerheads with this evil among us let us expect a miracle and nothing less but let our faith outgrow our need for a miracle. We have our own thoughts about the card of pain but God owns the deck.

However, unlike Mephibosheth, we are called to get out of our shells of fear and uncertainty for it is in fear that hesitation inhabits and in turn hesitation causes one's fear to become a living reality. There are riddles in this life that we can not change and puzzles we can not solve by immersing our sorry selves into the hopes of the sweet by and by to be experienced by the yet unconfirmed or unnamed 'not so many'. The reality we can not change should not be a boil in our bowels instead this should be a place where we accept that which we can not change and lean to the one who can change it by His might, Jesus Christ the lamb without blemish, God in flesh. It is in this level that we gain the serenity to get to grips with the unalterable parts of our spiritual journey through this natural habitat.

In life there are both tiny and enormous problems we all can not change and sometimes death is one of them for it is a law established as a result of Adam and Eve's fall but Paul comes to the rescue by saying 'to live is Christ and to die is gain'. However some of the pained like Mephibosheth suffer from mediocrace, the mental disease of not expecting much from ourselves. Our words like Mephibosheth's reflect the deeper thoughts of a defeated, conquered mind and our inner beings reflect the gloomy future so headed. It reflects a mentality filled with words of routed people:

"Such a dead dog as I am..."

Something in us should rise up, tingle within us, unsettle and take control of our every day situation so that we may by the grace of our lord Jesus Christ have an urgency to realize and establish a mentality that erases our calamities.

In essence it is in this pain that we behold that which scripture says 'eye has not seen'. It is in this suffering that we are set on a pilgrimage to realizing that which scripture says 'ear has not heard' and it is in these calamities that we turn ahead the hands of time and peep through the window of the unseen future in an unfailing endeavor to perceive that which scripture says 'neither has the heart of men perceived what the lord has prepared for those who love Him'.

Suffering should get in to our inner minds and extremely be focused on and seen as a shadow and a definite reality for both the Christian and for the present ailing world so let us have hope beyond the present. In essence there inhabits in pain many and awesome lessons of life than there are in the lips of joy but neither a dog nor a dead dog can realize it. Let us not have an Israelite mentality of failing to see beyond manna. There is breakthrough in the grill; just wait, for it is not the swift who shall win the race but those who endure.

Only a mind that dares to be very different can find the lessons and only a believer who refuses with all their might to be just a believer will definitely without fail find the treasures of this pain and this suffering, the gospel the church forgot to preach…

CHAPTER THREE

OUTCH! THAT HURTS

Job's life spirals down before him shattered by whispers of visage-less forces. The stereotype domesticity in his conscience conjures him to erect a permanent decision for a temporary circumstance. His lack of condor profoundly demolishes the entire propensity to identify God in the midst of heaven's silence. Even the dark mist that overshadows his mentality deters him from realising heaven where the inaugural scenes of his life endeavours are set, recorded, analysed and where the blue print of the author of his own life and faith inhabits. Job's pain is alive!

Buried in the bosom of Job's subconscious mind are the unsung verses of his life. They are dangling in the spiritual realm, gazing at him from afar and only God can alter, visualise or read them. Only God can offer Job a chance to peep through the colossal veil that separates the immortal from the mortal but it seems God is simply not in a fastidious frame of mind. He is the only one with the upper hand; Job is nothing more than a fleck of ground loom and his suggestions are neither required nor assumed. He is in the dock of pain and suffering, found guilty by forces that consume every hope of an acquittal. Like many of us Job journeys through this oblique midnight process of faith where to him God punishes but chooses to remain anonymous. He is not acquainted with the opening scenes of his life endeavours. The script is in heaven and Job is on earth hence he adjured for an answer: "Why do you hide your face?" but God is silent and as for the question, it is simply not answered.

Job is never accorded a dispensation to draw back the portiere, go behind the scenes to heed the devil impeaching him of self-seeking in his apparent piety. The devil infers that Job is a hypocrite and Job is neither a guest of honour, nor even a jar bearer at this rendezvous, like the rest of the afflicted he is here on earth, suffering, and God and the devil are in heaven. All the silence that he experiences in the midst of his battles is triggered by this unseen rendezvous in the snow-white fluffy clouds of heaven and surprisingly enough God is the detonation stratagem:

> "Hast thou considered my servant Job...?"
> [Job 1 vs. 8]

What! Have I heard correctly? Yes, it is God who pens down the first paragraph leading to Job's suffering pages; He proof reads it, copy edits and rewrites the chapters surrounding his life. Job is still grounded here on earth, suffering, yet God is in Heaven. What Job only understands is his regrettable life has been profoundly ushered in to oblivion, PERIOD. The contrast however is God being God might be understanding pain from both points of view, heaven's and earth's. Job like all suffering people only understands pain and suffering from an earthly point of view where pain can never be a valuable agent to anything. Is Job's definition of pain and suffering the same as God's? We infer not, since there is no real panoramic view of this thought but the whole book of Job must have the answer either to substantiate this view or dump it and focus on other plausible raison d'être why it is thus.

Job peeps through the window of abundant opportunities, visualised what seemed to be his only destiny - death, but could not interpret the unsung verses embedded in the very core of the inner man, the spirit man. There is a flare smouldering inside of him, ingesting up the optimism of a new painless crack of dawn. Job is not within the peripheral of what will only give him solace. He is unaware of what happens in heaven and the sheer knowledge of a God who can stop pain but is not stopping it seems to be an imminent boil within his armpits. He can not embody his suffering. We have to understand Mr Job, he had walked with God as if there was no sign of a morrow and had managed his riches as if there was, but now like every afflicted being, he was now swallowing poignant juice. He cries for an irreversible situation to be reversed. He imprudently asks rhetoric questions.

> "Why was I not hidden in the ground like a still born child, like an infant who never saw the light of day…" [Job 3 vs. 16]

THE CONFUSION

The book of Job seems more of God's curriculum vitae than a true story of suffering and pain. In it God seems to give Himself a period to share His immeasurable abilities and countless supremacy to a dysfunctional, flux smelling, leprosy swamped, and bed ridden Mr Job. Mrs Job waits, cries, advises Job and watches as the lessons commence, she is not also aware of the scene in heaven only God and the devil know. They, God and the devil are in heaven and Job is the subject matter of their theological argument. To Mr Job, the almighty God's lessons span from snow being hidden in the blankets of the highest mountains to the wild goats giving birth. One might as well say alas to the book, put up the shutters, close it and slither behind the dark recesses of their own minds.

The book of Job is a script of less answers and plenty questions. As a matter of fact Job as a name means 'Where is my father?' Within the cries of his being lies a name crying to be addressed and a void begging to be filled. The name 'Job' or Iyyob in Hebrew and Job himself are crying – Where are you God?

Despite the defunct theological depiction of the book of Job being a lesson of pain, I have come across it to be a ready manual parading a God who says 'I can do what I want, run the world the way I like' More so God adamantly does or seems not to offer any apparent answer to the quandary of pain in this story. Only a retort far lack of a clear answer is provided. The book as a whole focuses on the equivocations of Job, blames his friends, records his losses, points at Mrs Job's lack of intellectual elucidation with regards to the family dilemma and expectably feels Job's pain. At the end one feels they are nowhere in the vicinity of the solution in chapter forty two as in the foremost chapters BUT maybe we might dig a bullion colliery of lessons within the murky pages of this seemingly answerless book.

Pain and suffering with their chains hoist a lot of issues on the almightiness of God for instance how can Job reconcile the scripture that claims 'with God all things are possible' with all that he sees within the boundaries set before him explaining otherwise? How can he identify with a God who says He loves yet does not foil pain, let alone eradicate it?

It can be implied however by other pundits that what we think plausible with the finite wits is really zilch compared to the infinite God's definition of it and more to this superlative ideal might lie the potentiality of God not more concerned enough about how and what we think of him not solving this diabolic puzzle we face in our excruciating lives than us triumphing. Again to the marginal 'others' it is said the rejoin to pain and suffering lies not in Job's realization of God's purpose in all this trial but on the definitions in the wording of scripture and to be stern enough, in our mistranslating and perceptiveness of them. That is to suggest God being able to do 'everything' might not mean the nonsensical smidgens and pieces of 'everything.'

As an exemplar God can be vital without being hearty, peaceful without being idle, excluding love without sentimentality, testing without tempting, modest yet authoritative, loves the sinner without loving the sin, sometimes dictates without being a dictator and holds the ability to do everything without Him doing the aberrant within the 'everything'. This is further evidenced by the free will limitations the creature has as compared to the creator. With this free will we can never slay God if we wanted but if free will connotes 'free will' as our definition depicts then we can do what we want and this means we can do the former without any complications but our failing to do what we want despite the fact that we have this 'free will' is lucid evidence that our definitions are immensely flawed and necessitate great connotations, if not a far-reaching annihilation of them. In a nutshell there are possible limitations to everything possible.

In this book of Job, what Mr. Job suffers might simply be an aspect of bringing him to that sagacious good that lies within the possible 'everything' that God 'can' do but for Job to be the 'dys' within the function of the devil he has to understand that there are things God 'can not do' not because He can not do them but because He makes or has made Himself unable to do them and critically for the reason that by doing them He will be forced to do that which is divinely uncharacteristic (going against His own word which God will never do). For God to be able to leave Job's free will intact He has to abstain from predestining Job's every rejoinder to the devil's temptations. Paul's letter to Titus confirms that God can not lie so if our definition of 'God being able to do everything' means 'unreservedly everything' then we have to alter it to the 'everything' that is defined within the vocabulary of God and not our own flawed one. The difference we see is nothing short of a language barrier between God and Job; Job seems to stringently speak 'earth' where God speaks 'heaven', Oh! My!

Our conception of God should be driven by a revelation of who He really is and how He defines that which will always remain relevant to us. This part remains the first and burly hurdle to the problem of pain and the enigma of why we suffer. We should therefore erase the dim conception that defines God as a corrupt judge with a humanly passive principle of mercy where everything is done our way and not God's way or definition. We should preach the God of love to those in the pew without forgetting the God of war He is. For Job to move up the stepladder of this conundrum of pain he has to take no notice of the demonic eloquence of his darling, Mrs. Job, try and move beyond pain by leaving God to be God because omnipotence to him and to us for that matter, might be a diminutive silhouette of what God says it is. Job's definition of love amidst suffering should not remain inconsequential if he wants 'out'; in fact it should be piloted by a heavenly dimension that regulates how this love is made perfect in the vista of God.

MOVING BEYOND PAIN

Underpinning Job's logomachies is that unequivocal quintessence of faith in God and a realisation of the might of God. In spite of all the unbridled contention, and trust in God's justice; Job reposed on the pillar of hope stretched out to the helm of happiness of a distant resurrection, gazed towards the future vindication and recognised a God who was in control and who defined pain in a vocabulary far different to his and far from the reach of his kindred, including Mrs Job. He slipped and dovetailed Apostle Paul's exclamation 'For our light affliction, which is *just for a moment*, worketh for us a far more exceeding and eternal weight of glory; While we look not at the things which are seen, but at the things which are not seen: for the things that are seen are temporal; but the things which are not seen are eternal' (Italics: mine).

He identified the extraordinary, went beyond it to become the pain of 'pain', scaled above it and became lager than life itself. Through the realms of illuminating space of anguish, Job avowed God and the ordained destiny, his in particular.

> "Naked came I out of my mother's womb naked shall I return: the Lord gave and Lord hath taken away, blessed is the name of the Lord..." [Job 1 vs. 21]

In acceding to pain as the decree of God, Job revamped his conscience and freed himself from the slavery of pain. Physically he was still buffeted by the acute episodes of this suffering perdition but spiritually he was absent from its vicinity with the anticipation of a sanctified life somewhere further than the present. Job's masculine glorification of a seemingly hushed God in the midst of his pain enacts the pinna of Eloim's ears. It builds a non argumentative boldness to humble himself (Job) before the Almighty God. It might seem vague that even if he has done the 'humbleness' business, pain and suffering still engulf him. He might howl again:

> "Why was I not hidden in the ground like a still born child, like an infant who never saw the light of day..." [Job 3 vs. 16]

Giving up the ghost might have appeared imminent but his faith made him conscious of life beyond entombment. It orchestrated a God inhabited heart full of unadulterated anticipation even in the dirge of anguish. Faith here embodies an element of fear and respect for God. The trepidation of considering another approaching day whilst in that equivalent anguish made him morbid but the conviction of trouncing the repression of pain and suffering kept him keeping on. This fervour assists every sufferer to identify with the certainty that personal and spiritual conflicts are resolved by adopting a fierce morale inventory; making a rock solid commitment to accept and consider the veracity of those things we cannot transform and those that we can by yielding all to Christ.

Job understood the consequences of his logomachies; thoughts raised against your redeemer will only muzzle the limb that redeems. He faced the reality of pain by going through it and ultimately beyond it. He left God to delineate the pages of his life which seemed to him unexplainable. It is in this type of mind that God's hand is moved; when people leave God to be God.

Complacence was not Job's greatest choice either, it was his desire to comprehend the degree of humility accepted by God - letting God's will above our own, for it is the will of God on earth that works not Job's will in heaven. By this deportment he overpowered the concealed voice of the prowler functioning in the twilight locale of power, lobbying his diabolic course on him and Job accepted his suffering with all its clutches as a "would be history" not a "would be everyday life".

The author of Job's life story presents, a cross-grained patch Job journeyed through, in-between the horns of a dilemma: one negative and one positive. Satan is in full force to destroy Job and God is using His omnipotent abilities to freeze His omniscience concerning Job's love towards Him and testing him at the same time. Remember God is not an impassive remote control; He knows Job's love is genuine. He is not dramatising Job's life, so He grants Job free will. The devil tempts, God is testing, Job is weeping and his hope is dwindling with every test within the abridgement of the story:

> "Cursed is the day I was born"

Job goes on:

> "Though the lord slays me yet will I trust in him..."

Job's above assertion is a direct proof that though everything in the scriptures is divinely inspired it might not necessarily be a *statement of truth* (please get me right on this): e.g. God never tried to slay Job yet we find this lie coming out of Job's mouth recorded within scripture and that does not make the Bible flawed but adds to its reliability since it records all the good and the bad sayings of its characters, it gives us a prayerful David and in other verses records his greatest sins. Its purpose is to exhibit the thoughts of those like you and me who have a relationship with an infinite God who only seems to understand pain from heaven's point of view. In this juncture it is not required of God to change his perception concerning some of the most troubling definitions, but it is commanded of us by the word of this same God to have '...the mind which was also in the lord Jesus Christ...' by so doing we finetune into the frequency of God and begin to employ the vocabulary that He Himself uses in defining love, pain, suffering and omnipotence.

We can not hide the fact that every sufferer wants God in the dock, to ask him questions and even jilt him to the core. It is humanity's wish to put God in the answering chair were he can elucidate the now unexplainable, the now answerless and maybe punish Him by making him drink His own medicine. Job pleaded for this prospect, he says, "Even to day is my complaint bitter: my stroke is heavier than my groaning. Oh if I knew where I might find Him! That I might come even to His seat! I would order my cause before him, and fill my mouth with arguments. I would know the words which He would answer me, and understand what He would say unto me" We would think by the above words Job is abandoning God yet the second line in his tautology says of God, "...He would put strength in me..."

Job's continuing wording of his pain if not His state of mind as a sufferer and the beauty of pain is shown within the words of his own mouth. Pain most of the time (to me as an author it seems like all the time) seems to build a better character. This analysis is further analysed and agreed upon by C.S Lewis when he talks about pain by uttering the words:

> "I am not convinced that suffering...has any natural tendency to produce such evils [anger and cynicism]. I did not find the front line trenches of the C.C.S. more full of hatred, selfishness, rebellion, and dishonesty than any other place. I have seen great beauty of spirit in some who were great sufferers. I have seen men, for the most part, grow better not worse with advancing years, and I have seen the last illness produce treasures of fortitude and meekness from most unpromising subjects...If the pain is indeed a 'vale of soul making,' it seems on the whole to be doing its work"

It seems to me pain is back on the payroll more often than not. Many 'pain paraphernalia' writers and theologians have found pain to turn people to God more than pure happiness does. It is a simple fact of life that can not be denied though we might try to twirl the reality of the facts in our own facades. It is true that pain serves a lot in a believer's life. First it is said to 'burn out the dross,' or distil us and lead us to greater holiness of life. But it is also proven that it can 'burn in the promises,' or lead us to closer dependence on God and his faithful promises to us. Burn it will – but look also at what the burning is for.

THE DEVIL DOESN'T KNOW SQUAT!

The devil's adventure is not impromptu or ad-lib, he is swimming in the sea of his own lust and innuendos. He can only infer Job doesn't love God for nought, he cannot see Job's thoughts, only God can since He is omniscient.

Note: when God says "hast thou considered my servant Job that there is none like him in the earth, a perfect and an upright man- one that feareth the Lord and esweth evil". Satan was latently quick to display his lack of knowledge "doth Job fear (you) God for nought... thou hast blessed the work of his hands, put forth your hand now, and touch (destroy) all that"

He searches for every practical opportunity to discern Job's thoughts and his love for God. At the tempting of Christ, the devil inquires 'if thou be the son of God change these stones into bread, He is always looking for a practical way to prove what he has heard us saying. He is that foolish to such an extend that he could not really understand Jesus was actually God. After the event at Calvary he says 'if we had known we would not have crucified...' (Author's paraphrase). The devil is not all knowing, he is simply a spiritually dead unemployed cherub.

The author of Job reaches in-between the lines and deduces the ultimate truth that no one can have control over Job and every believer for that matter except it is given him from above.

Note: even the devil has to ask for permission to mess with your life, again note that the devil is not only attempting to obliterate Job's life but is also trying to make God responsible for the action, "put forth your hand and touch all that..." but God is a good God, He will not just spew bad tidings to His beloved children. He is aware of the prowler. God knows Job will overcome so allows the devil to do all that he can, "and the Lord said unto Satan, behold he (Job) is in thine hands, *except his life*" (Italics and bold: mine).

Calamities will never lean on the bosom of your present or future unless God meant them for His divine purposes. If they have God's blueprint then rejoice and like the philosopher Solomon says:

> "...who can make straighten that which He (God) has made crooked? In the day of prosperity be joyful, but in the day of adversity consider: God also hath set the one over against the other...
> [Eccl 13 vs. 13-14]

Consider, for all things no matter how bad work for the good of all those who love God. Note the word says God has set and not created. God only allows, He does not cause evil so wait (pray without seizing, that is to wait upon) upon Him to complete that which He purposed through pain and suffering. If you wait upon the will of the Lord, no weapon yielded against you shall prosper, even if the devil upbraids you he still doesn't know you the way that God does. Again note: The word only says "won't prosper" he never said the weapon will neither be yielded nor did he say touch you, He is simply saying though it might touch you it will never prosper (overcome you). See, we should all be meticulous when reading the word so we do not miss any important revelation or choke it.

THE THIEF OF TIME

Never procrastinate pain. Procrastination is the thief of time and the accumulator of pain. Job never adjourned it; he just went through it and obtained a breakthrough. If you procrastinate and adjourn pain you will suffer more than necessary. It must be understood in the very generic sense that we should never waste the present by struggling to put in reverse gear that which can be achieved by the front gear. Job heard of the destruction and fell on his knees and spoke

"The Lord gave and the Lord has taken away,
Blessed be the name of the Lord"

In his suffering he moved from a painful trial to an appositive testimony, ran away from self exaltation for he had no ground for it. His test became a testimony. The choice to praise God in the middle of a storm determined his destiny. Job realised that for him to tap into the unsearchable riches and grace of God he had to surrender both, soul and spirit to be guided by divine might.

Many believers do not consider pain thereby depicting a contrast between God's way and our way. A way which demolishes the promotion of a receptive mind rids us of a 'spiritual mastiff' attitude of demising to pain and refusing to surmount pain. If we are willing to prevail over pain, we have to be convinced of the truth beyond pain and beyond reasonable doubt, manifest it in life and death. Like Job let us seize the moment and tune into the frequency of the God who sometimes seems silent and sometimes is silent.

Keep in mind that every believer who suffers before its necessary suffers more than is necessary. It is never enough to possess a sound mind, the main thing is to employ it and Job can only employ it by living in the present. His case is in the hands of the great 'I AM' and if Job tries to live in the past by engrossing his mind within the pains of yesterday he will miss his redeemer for He lives in the present and not the past. If he tries to live in the future there is a problem again in that though God sees the future He does not live in it for He is a God of the now so Job should realise the presence of God in his suffering and how he is going to redeem him in the 'today' of his life and not the 'yesterday'.

GOD'S MODOS OPERANDI

Without resorting to religious and doctrinal cannibalism as well as drosinism, God's modos operandi (the way He meets a specific need) is different to what we always perceive. There is a daunting juncture when He breaks the numbing pain:

> "Who is that, that darkens my counsel by words without knowledge...where were you when I laid the foundation of the earth?"
> [Job 38 vs. 2, 4]

God's response to Job heralds the limit of our finite minds; it begets the exposure of the magnitude of torment we will have effectuated by godless cantankerous contentions and by our malfunction as sufferers in surmounting the suffering we go through. God breaks His silence in a great compelling glow that is shinier than we can embody let alone expect. God shows that all these empty words that Job/sufferers said were gate crushing heaven and falling on His ears. He heard Job, however He did not answer him in an egalitarian vogue for He is not obligated to do our will but His - painful and graphic but factual. We might have the licence to rule over this earth and might pray to God to transfer that license to him here and there as we have seen in the previous chapter but let us not forget that for God to take that license; our needs have to line with His will. God is not obligated to do anything outside His own will.

For Job to say "I will complain in the bitterness of my soul" is to cancel the real facts. It is synonymous with inducing God as reprehensible whereas He is perpetually inerrant and eternally sufficient. Job's tautology can never be justified; he has vitiated God's council by hypothesising that he "would complain" to God as if it was right. Rueful as it is, no one can subvert the subway of grace by telling God when, how and to whom shall grace be given.

These over simplified theologies create a sufferer not a conqueror. Life to the sufferer is less than the mirth of derision which engulfs every fibre of thought and at most ushers the pained to the only escape button; blaming God. It is well weighed to take note that almost any pain Job went through, he went quicker than the way he surmounted. What Job failed to do at first was to drop the drooling pain of the yester-hours and realise that today and the morrow were planted within the womb of an 'I AM' God who lives in the present, sees the future in the present as clearly as he will have seen the yester.

The friends of Job's tautologies are a mere shadow of the reality of God. They shed a picture of a God who punishes, their point and reason of pain is nothing more than Job's sins. To them what he was experiencing was a justified punishment from a judgemental God. How far were they from the truth! It is seen by their analogy of the whole story of their friend Job that there are people in our company who will give us all sorts of ideas and ideals but these may not be the things we so need in our pain. They turned into just fault finders in a faultless character. All the chapters of their tautology turned to me like the longest way of saying absolutely nothing.

It is said anyway that nothing is easier found than fault – finding; no talent, no revelation, no self denial, no brains and no character are required to set up in this grumbling business. Faults are mostly viewed like head lights of a motionless vehicle: those of others seem more glaring than our own. Taking this head on, there is a lot friends, relatives, guardians or spouses who will have suggestions especially on the 'whys', when we are deep in pain but it is a sane mind that questions almost every suggestion, for in many suggestions lie a degree of assumed fault. People usually give advice after finding fault but there are others who simply thrive on kangaroo auditing so stroke off those that only focus on your faults but cling so ever tightly to those that after pointing the faults remain to be part of the solution and part of the breakthrough.

Friends with a vision will always show you where to find that important spyglass to gaze the heavens in search of those unsung verses. Job's failure to spot the unsung verses of his life led him to lament even the day of his birth.

> "Let the day perish wherein I was born, and
> the night In which it was said, There is a man
> (Job) conceived"

He reversed instead of advancing. He drowned himself in the joy to be gained in the distant 'sweet by and by', in the reality of this present shadow, the world. Job at first did not have a dream of his predicament being fixed within his present life. He opened his mouth to speak:

> "I know that my redeemer lives, and that in
> the end He will stand upon the earth. And
> after my skin has been destroyed, yet in my
> flesh I will see God; I myself will see him
> with my own eyes…I, and not another. How
> my heart yeans within me!" [Job 19:25-27]

WHEN GOD WHEN?

It is hard to know how, 'the good', whatever it is ,whenever it will come and whatever it looks like will manage to sooth all the wounds the suffering experienced caused. The level of comfort this 'good' brings is not only a guess or a hope we, as humans arbour so as to escape the ugly realities of pain but a lantern on the stern for all who are in pain. Though only God knows how he wants us to react to this counterbalance there is no one among us that can weigh what effect this 'good' has on a pained soul. Only God and the sufferer will ever know.

Existing between fiction and reality is the state of a suffering person. The stupid, weak, petty and unfruitful solutions and promises of a breakthrough from peers brace our ears. The deacon, the teacher, the friend and the claiming 'prophet' that once visited seem to have lost the address to your home, your phone never rings. The visiting Pastor's voice has gained a tremor that is when the question 'when God when?' rings.

Since I do not write to ease the logical compulsions inside my mind, I have to admit that the feelings, if not revelations obtained and placed watchfully in these pages have been received after own experiences that I promised not to mention for the fear of them being repugnant and at most not in line with some parts of my suffering audience. The questions why? and when God when? will always ring no matter what your social, political or theological status is.

Even Job reached the uttermost depth of pain to the level he had to tell God:

> "What is man that make so much of him, that you give him so much attention, that you examine him every morning and test him every moment? Will you never look away from me, or let me alone even for an instant?"
> [Job 7:17-18]

Job just wanted to be left alone even for a moment as his

request entails yet God keeps on keeping on. He is trying to make ends meet but every time they are about to meet, it seems God moves the ends so he pleads to be left alone. This is all because though he knew sometime in his life a breakthrough might come, he could not perceive the time when his pain will all be over. He wanted a day, hour and minute but God did not provide him with them, not even with a decade. Behind this tautology of a pained Job is the painful stand of a more than rhetoric question 'When God when?'

But when God will heal the scars is a question only God can answer not us. If we do not have an answer to this then let us accept the fact that we can not do anything concerning knowing the time God will work a miracle in us to get us out of the present predicament and then move on with life but let us never quit on trusting God. This lack of knowledge of the 'when?' and the 'how?' is another clear limitation of what I discussed about, the 'free will' factor. It is God's principle for us to pass through these trials on our way to meet the divine call without us acting as mere nod heads and him, a passive remote control.

Remember even Christ needed to be crossed first before he received a crown. We are the light of the world so in order to provide that light we should endure burning! Oh! My!

CHAPTER FOUR

AWAKENING A SLEEPING GOD

Notice Joseph in the field of roses? He is that certain other thorn beneath the stem of a withered flame lily.

> "And Joseph was brought down to Egypt and Portifar an officer of Pharaoh, captain of the guard, an Egyptian bought him off the hand of the Ishamaelites, which had brought him down thither" [Genesis 39 vs. 1]

He is the one sliding down the razor blade of emotions. When dreams arise, he holds ever so tightly through the cold and lonely nights, only to wake up with empty hands embracing Portifar's cosy couch. It seems bona fide yet it is just a bundle of meagre chaff the Devil hijacked and bagged. Just an unfunny joke and a filthy gag the devil fermented. A Jerusalem he once adored has hard-pressed him into a pamphlet of a poisoned Egypt. Even his repulsive screams haunt him in his nightmares. What a dead rub?

Joseph is pacing through the Via Dolorosa of his suffering

life paragraphed by hades' biros and created by the egocentrism of his own brothers and more so, the slave-thirst Ishmaelites. He is deep in the Marie Claire, way at the end of his rope. Groaning within him is a call for a dedicated divine pair of pliers to cut him loose from this thud of pain. He had answered when nature called, now emotional dilemma has impelled him to drown into the abyss of the quicksand of anguish and the well of unfathomable suffering. In his guises to noticeably acclimatize to the changing phizogs of Egypt, he expects an appalling panic attack but faith in God leads him to the denial of self.

Joseph's summer is dwindling but he can not consent to his season vanishing without a trace. Can this be that part of hades where a silent and mute God hurls a snowball that quenches the diabolic flames of hell? He lingers and finally enquires of Portifar's dreams for his mansion, inserting Portifar's dreams above his own. Only now can the pangs of pain ease. He surely must have moved the hand of the unmoving God through abolishing self centeredness (egocentric):

> "…and he (Portifar) made him overseer over his house, and all that he had he put into his hands." [Genesis 39 vs. 4]

Pain is a monster that shifts with an adaptation of a mind that breaks away from that diabolic sense of egocentric tendencies. The moment our minds take on board a sense of placing other people's needs and hopes above our own, that monster loses its form and its very venom to paralyse our hope for a breakthrough. Though it is agreed upon and proven that pain bears many facets, this principle will move and erase one of the major set backs we face in all our suffering times.

THE MANY FACES OF EVIL
Primmer Donna fatigue never robbed Joseph of his better judgement. He had been raised by the godly hand of his frail, old and dying father Jacob, back in Canaan, far from its great jutting moor lands and away from its madding crowds. The teaming terraces of Egypt and its well manicured turfs and the ever so ugly awaiting experiences were just but an invitation to a higher calling disguised in slavery, rape charges, unfounded verdicts and long jail sentences.

Jacob, his father had lectured to him on the ingredients of preparing a delicious and formidable recipe to spice up and put in motion the hand of the living God and it was now Joseph's time and call to prepare his superlative dish. A clear cut period to put his own dreams to a halt and concentrate on making other people's dreams become a reality. It is working but not for long.

> "And she caught him by his hand saying, lie with me: and he (Joseph) left his garment in her hand and fled…and…she called unto the men of her house…and saying he (Joseph) came in unto me and lie with me, and …left his garment with me and fled…and Joseph's master put him in prison [Genesis 39 vs. 12, 14, and 15]

Sometimes, somehow, in the middle of no man's land- we are caught up in circumstances beyond our own control. We are bound by chains we know not which and our eyes are seldom dry. In it we dawdle and dither with the hope that our provision will provide the vision yet the vision of fulfilling other people's dreams before ours will in itself be a divine path to provide the so needed provision of being released from the chains of a jail, pain and suffering.

This is a time not to get stuck with the chains of one

particular step of our lives. Every step whether joyful or tormenting, is designed by a loving God to get us to the next level in the accomplishment of fulfilling our divine destiny. It is not what God is doing *to* Joseph but what God is doing *for* Joseph that matters and that is my unending focus as the author.

However, the promise of a higher power mightier than any mortal or immortal soothing the fists of sound looms high but before we know it, we are back in the abyss of quadrupled anguish. Where is the vision? We ask but the answer must have bypassed us, eluded us somewhere between the streets of hope and the avenues of reality. It is in this period of incommode and twinge that we are called to ignore our very own anguish by first ministering to others' pangs of pain and suffering; a time for the denial of self. A moment of demolishing the egocentric syndrome buried in the Joseph of our hearts. It will be a definite season to surmount the 'me' factor and gaze at the 'you' aspect.

When circumstances shallow the arenas of mankind's lair, pain reminds us of the wealthiness and diversity of our existence. It might seem like Joseph has become an item of derision but his wings are ready and positioned to please where he travels and travel where he pleases. To the 'analytical bowl' over the edges of my shoulder - Joseph is descending but to the reality of realities of scripture he is ascending for:

"The Lord was with Joseph..." [Genesis 39 vs. 2]

He knows silence rarely means absence but still, despair bolts his doors; he is speaking to long gone stone walls with a loo chamber for a head rest, sleeping besides a slumbering cup bearer and subjected to the unwelcome snoring of a dozing baker. He is in a kingly prison but the very fact of being its inhabitant comes out of a lethal price. Joseph is worse than the other two prisoners, his is a rape case. In a nutshell, he is one of Pharaoh's worst enemies and the jury's verdict always runs in pursuit of guillotine. BUT;

HOLD ON!

His stance of self denial is not a turning loose of emotion, but an escape from mal faith and a reaching out to the unfathomable depth of the substance for what he hoped for. It is an exhibit for things not yet seen. He would rather stand in akimbo before the gruesome and sharpened guillotines of Egypt than gain 'self' or rather keep it. He has just begun but God's silence is still a boil deep down in his armpits and a wound bound within his mind. The prayers he wishes answered are not answered. To him his prayer words are empty gongs that ricochet at the granite ceiling of smelling and hideous prison cells.

Hear me! All sufferers like Joseph, are mere petals folded within the core of the lily. Their scent is hidden until their minds are freed to hearing a silent God in the midst of a storm. The fact remains however they all have a scent so beautiful it has to be unfolded, for many it is just by a paradigm shift. God weaves His threads of enlightenment through a sufferer's mind with the clearest threads that make them understand, appreciate and realise their scent. Though they might not perceive it, smell their scent or see God work through their pain and suffering, the truth is on the table, He is and vitally they have a scent.

BEHOLD!

Behold a tailor stands with the threads of pain behind all our lives, we should let Him do his work, see Him through His expertise, find a way to have patience for the work will soon be finished and we will all be adorned with beauty booming with scent and clothed in awe. Not in the distant 'sweet by and by' but in the sweet 'now and now'.

God knows what He is tailoring in us through the agency of pain and suffering. Please let Him be. Instead of asking the question 'Is God silent?' let us ask this question 'Am I the silent and mistaken one?' Joseph did it, realised God was not at all silent and it worked for him to the extent that he ended up running the whole of the Egyptian economy. Patience and temperance will always work! And your scent will always be in the open.

Behold He is working! The tailor is tailoring. Leave Him be.

GOD DOES NOT FORESEE, HE SEES.

God sees the present and the future as clearly as the past and to Him what you are afraid of has already happened or has already been prevented that is why Jesus only healed one cripple at the pool of Bethsaida. He had already seen the others jump into the pool of Bethsaida and get healed so to him that problem had already been solved. He had seen it in the future as clearly as he sees both the present and the past. What the suffering audience fail to see often is God does not foresee the future, He sees it.

The Lord who defines the future from the beginning is a Lord indeed. With him we become assured of the certainty of the future and the reality of the morrow unseen. In Him the uncertain certainty becomes evidently certain. He knows all our morrows so why should we whimper about the present pain and suffering? He has all the power and majesty to change our future. Why not let Him do the best? He can see the future so why not pray to Him who has the keys to change or alter it?

THE PRISON OF THE MIND

Do you feel like you are a prisoner? Then there is no dungeon as dark as one's own heart! No jailer is as inexorable as one's self. You are sitting on a call and a God given gift to abolish 'self' and be able to survive life in the hardest concentration camps brewed even by Hades' chief demons. Enquire of the dreams of those around you, fulfil them first before yours and in the end you will move the hand of a seemingly silent and seemingly unconcerned God. Like Joseph you become a vessel ready for the master's use. This truth should drown deep inside the bones of the inner 'you' for without it many have blamed God for divers misfortunes. Many a time it is this lack of knowledge and wisdom that causes and grabs us into the iron chains of suffering and pain's serfdom. God does not blame himself on this; instead He says 'my people perish because of lack of knowledge'. Joseph has the knowledge he even enquires of the jailer's dream for the jail he is in as proof he had the principle of self denial buried deep inside him and:

> "...The keeper of the prison committed to Joseph's hand all the prisoners that were in prison; and whatsoever they did there; he was the doer of it. The keeper of the prisoner looked not to anything that was under his hand [Genesis 39 vs. 22-23]

How degrading and unwelcome it must have been for Pharaoh ex-chief cup bearer, the baker and all the prisoners to be placed under the hand of a 'rapist'. If I was there I would have been the first prisoner to object to Joseph's leadership, just felt I should testify. This however comes to me as proof that God will make you a leader in a much unexpected place if you remain focused on your goal like Joseph was. Though he did not commit the crime, all the convicts regarded him as a rapist who forced Portifar's wife to bed and to leave him in charge of inmates of all genders would be like leaving candy around a hungry toddler-more so;

scripture tells us that "the keeper of the prison looked not to anything that was under his hand". Joseph was in total control with regards the prison logistics and all that was under his hand. What a place to be in control yet God is not at all slowing down.

Joseph's call is not to trespass on his jail inmates' solitude but only to place their interests before his. He is trading in areas and dungeons where the pained and the suffering like you and I seldom trade. Normally a sufferer would be sitting miserably in the corner of a certain solitary confinement trying to search for excuses to blame God for the entire predicament suffered. Joseph is different. Within half of no time the baker sighs and wakes from the penumbra of sleep and so does the cup bearer, and both have bothering dreams and Joseph is ready. He is set to do his divine duty. Ready to fulfil his call- the call to fulfil other people's dreams first, before his own.

> "...And Joseph said unto them...tell me then (Your dreams), I pray you. [Genesis 40 vs. 8]

Can you see the ghostly glow of a lonely morning loitering in front of Joseph's cell? Can you hear the thick winds from the burning sand dunes of the Egyptian deserts enveloping his cell? Joseph answers the baker and the cup bearer's dreams. I can see Joseph's left hand resting on the baker's collarbone comforting him. The other is shaking the butler's hand. You would unambiguously assume that his time for a breakthrough is upon him, now and maybe only now can he ask to be remembered, but will he? At the end of his tether Joseph throws a plea:

> "But think on me when it shall be well with thee, and shew kindness, I pray thee, unto me and make mention of me unto Pharaoh

and bring me out of this house...and it came to pass...he (Pharaoh) restored the chief butler unto butlership...yet did...the butler remember Joseph, but forgat him [Genesis 40 vs. 14, 23]

Can you hear the 'adamant' walls of a royal jail still confronting Joseph with news of yet another time and summons of added pain and acute suffering? Sunshine is nigh but as is the case with every human, the 'helped' hastily forget and soon the helper's sunshine is near sunset but the idea is not to get angry when they forget but to rejoice forever more. Words of pain haunt Joseph but nothing can bring him down for he is on a divine call. He is on a divine call that defies all odds. He waits upon the God who reveals dreams to give him another soul with a dream to fulfil. God is not there when he needs him but he is always there on time when he interprets the dreams of others - soon Pharaoh has a dream; but this is after years. Where was God? And where is the butler?

"It came to pass...that pharaoh dreamed... and none could interpret...then spake the chief unto Pharaoh...there with us a young man, a Hebrew...he interpreted to us our dreams...then Pharaoh sent and called Joseph" [Genesis 41 vs. 1, 8, 11, 14]

MODES OPERANDI

God's modes operandi (the way He meets a need) is sometimes a tiresome, agonising and long rollercoaster ride through pain and suffering. He delights in believers who stand in the gap for strangers, warriors who stand the scrutiny of pain and time, and soldiers who ignore their own scars and delve into oncoming danger in an effort to shield others from the fiery darts of the devil. Many times when we are deep in this conflict with the devil about why we are helping others instead of ourselves, God, the sovereign Lord Himself sends His blessings to us without our immediate awareness but this will only come when a suffering person's expectation and trust in the omnipresent and omniscient God rises to the level they start to live what they proclaim. With this mind set, blessings will just be around the corner. All it sometimes needs is to show love by developing a character that denies 'self'.

As a matter of fact David under inspiration said 'pain may endure for a night but blessings come in the morning'. It does not matter to God how long your nights are going to be or how long they might have been but the principle point is mornings will always come. It never mattered to God how bad the demographics of Joseph's habitat were and how long his pain had taken and it surely does not matter how long you have suffered or will continue to suffer, what matters to God is whether you are fulfilling your divine destiny in that experience or not. It is not going to be long; nonetheless blessings are on their way. Our own lack of knowledge concerning the abolition of egocentric tendencies is usually the cause of catastrophes and not God.

It is all amazing how God really works. Joseph survived the hand of his brothers, the Ishmaelites, the wrath of Portifar and the uncomfortable quarters of an unforgiving and filthy Egyptian jail. The scripture in all the details it offers on the story of Joseph never talks of him ever having a single dream concerning his family in Canaan, but was made to fulfil even Pharaoh's dreams first before his.

> "And he (Pharaoh) made Joseph ruler over all the land of Egypt [Gen 41 vs. 43]

There he is a victorious Joseph, clad in kingly robes,

chariots around him, guards' eyes spare on him and the rule remains: To the victor belongs the spoils of the enemy. Denial of 'self' has made him triumph over adversity; he focused on the Saviour and never on the storm, on fulfilling strangers' dreams first before his own and now who can be against him. He is allowed everything in Egypt. The only thing he is not allowed is Pharaoh's wife. Who needs her anyway?

WHEN REVELATION COMES: SHUSH!

Tradition and revelation are always in conflict. Many sufferers have a jungle of ideas on what will get them out of a catastrophe yet God has His own plans on how you will come out of your own predicament be it self authored or devil made. It is as real as that. It is true that we wish we all have our testimonies heard before they get to full maturity, but if God does not confirm with your spirit that you need to tell it, don't. Christ said "...do not tell anyone who I am..." He knew that if His disciples started parading who He was to the people of his day and age He would have been crowned long before getting to the cross. Joseph kept who he was quiet to the ears of those surrounding him until the right time came when he was ruling the economy of all of Egypt. He new he had to suffer the pains of the cross before getting a crown.

In our journey through pain when we see the day of deliverance looming nigh let us shush our mouths, like Paul's letter to the Ephesians say; 'let us start speaking to ourselves in psalms', stop parading our expectations to those who might want to rush us into our destiny before we mature enough to carry it or those who might want to stop the divine path before us. Joseph, in all his trials is never recorded as having told Portiphar, the cup bearer, the baker or Pharaoh about the vision he had back at home. Instead, he kept assisting others as if it was his only destiny yet there was in him a great mission and commission waiting to be fulfilled and a gulf lingering to be stuffed.

Tradition would have wanted Joseph in all his trials to parade his call and destiny but revelation had God's blue print and it cried heavily unto him: "do not tell anyone who you are before you are fully mature to handle their reaction" (My own paraphrase). Joseph understood that a testimony is called a testi –mony because in it there is a 'mony' that comes out of the 'test' which means there should be a test first before you get a testimony and there is a mess before we all get a message; hence the Bible in Genesis says "There was darkness…and God said…"

What prepared Joseph for the power he finally assumed in Egypt was the utter pain of accusation, the suffering of having his brothers sell him off to the Ishmaelites, the suffering in an Egyptian jail and worst of all a wave of uncertainty on when this vision would become a reality. In a nutshell the test that Joseph had and passed catapulted him to greater heights of brake pedalling in to a breakthrough. It is not necessarily this pain that gave him a breakthrough but it was his response to pain and his perception of the problem he was experiencing that determined his future. The magnitude of his fight also determined the magnitude of his breakthrough. It seems clear to me that the greater the pain is, the greater the breakthrough. This might loom as being caused by the many lessons a suffering individual might have learnt during the times of adversity. Always sweet victory comes from a dreadful fight that's why Paul says:

>"…fight the good fight…" [1 Timothy 6 vs.12]]

THE GREATNESS OF TIMING

T.D. Jakes writes, in his book The Great Investment writes, "We wait for 'Mr Right' or 'Ms. Outta Sight.' We wait and we wait, then we begin to doubt that there is anyone out there for us. So we decide to have a little fun with 'Mr. Okay-For-Now,' and end up hurt and confused. Next we spend time with 'Ms. Too-Good-To-Be-True,' discover that she is, and leave with a broken heart and an empty wallet. 'Mr. Almost' and 'Ms. Pretty-Close' come along, but the more we get to know them, the further from our ideal they seem."

Many a time blessings lie in our ability to realise the presence of the Holy-Spirit. Timing as a divine principle: calls for a God inhabitant heart that can recognise the time, magnitude and power of the move of God. This principle on the importance of timing is strengthened by the scriptures where Elijah is in a cave at Mount Carmel and heard the powerful wind and thought God was in that wind but my Bible says God was not in that wind. The rumblings of an earthquake came to Elijah's ears and he assumed that God was in the earthquake but again my Bible says God was not in that earthquake. The third time He assumed God was in the flames of fire yet my Bible confirms God was not in that fire.

It was only until a small; still wind passed by that the scriptures said 'God was in that small wind'

It is common to miss the importance of timing which is deeply rooted in divine circles when we are in pain but there lies a great urgency in knowing the time, level and magnitude of God's Spirit. Do not get in to the rollercoaster of pain just because of this simple thing of failing to realise the great importance of timing. The great evangelists of past and present years like Kenneth Hagin, William Marrion Branham, A.A Allen, Benny Hinn, Oral Roberts, Chris Oyakhilome, Kenneth Copeland, Crefflo Dollar, Rodney Howard Browne, T.D. Jakes, Don Stewart and many more only prayed/pray for people when they sensed the presence of God. In fact Branham had a sure word that the angel of the Lord would be present, he needed to see him first in order to be sure of the will of God-That! Reader is real timing!

Though I do not wish to undermine Elijah, I also have to depict the truth of what happened in this instance. He could not at that time occlude to the principle of timing due to the suffering he was going through yet without this ability we are bound to live in anger, strife, physical and spiritual poverty. I as an author can understand why we might miss the move of God during pain but my analysis is not an excuse to miss this valuable piece of surmounting our quandary. It is a divine revelation to know that no one including me the message bearer can conquer what they can not confront in time. We must however be angry and do not get comfortable in our situation, be heavenly enraged about the circumstances around us, confront them in their rage, tell them without fail about our God and they will bow down to him.

Joseph found the balance between reality and the power of God. He realised the time of God's Spirit, a time of God's move and went through with it to win his wars in Egypt, miles away from home. Sometimes the best wars are won far away from the protective arms of those you know. I guess it is God's plan to get you to understand that He is the one that only matters when it gets to where the rubber meets the steel.

With all this in mind it is time to lay aside the filthy recesses of our brains, know the time of the move of the Holy-Spirit and slide down the deep of fulfilling other people's dreams before ours.

Never be ashamed of seeing your dreams running in pursuit of the dreams of those you helped for shame is the unstoppable clock of PRIDE. If you can see and perceive the time of God's move then you are right on track at least you can not suffer more than is necessary. It is all about the degree of timing you employ otherwise you might miss God's purpose in your life, follow your own ways and suffer as a result.

If we are called to look closely at the story of Joseph and at its theological meaning we will be directed to analysing the significance of a 'coat' in biblical times. A coat represented heirloom, honour and above all things favour. When Joseph was sold to the merchants by his brothers, the only coat he had was taken away from him, when he ran away from Portifar's wife the only coat he then owned was again taken away from him signifying Joseph's dwindling earthly favour. At every stage in Joseph's painful journey through life it seems every mortal was after the favour more than anything else but when the rollercoaster finally came to rest the only thing apart from the signet ring that he was presented with was a new coat, a kind of restored favour.

Within the edges of our lives and at every corner of time there are people running in pursuit of us either trying to take our favour from us or prevent us from using it to our gain but behind every web and mist of this painful life there stands a God who can restore everything.

THE ANOINTING

What would have happened if the baker and the cup bearer or Pharaoh for that matter had decided to interpret their own dreams?

There is a problem with people in this day and age that causes them to suffer before its necessary. One of the biggest problems is jumping into other people's anointing. Everyone wants to speak their own tongues, utter their own oracles, interpret their own tongues, teach their own sermon and prophesy their own lives all without the commission of God. Whilst it is very encouraged in the word to ask for these gifts, there is a great balance needed in understanding the scripture that says "not all prophesy..." There is need to know our limitations, know the level of our gifts as compared to those of other believers.

By this we might have a sure word on where to go when we need help, be it physical or spiritual. I am convinced you are aware of what would have happened if the baker and the cup bearer or Pharaoh had decided to interpret their own dreams.

If these ungodly individuals recognised the importance of spotting diversities in gifts and calling, how much can a Holy-Spirit filled people grow within the dimensions of God through recognising the differences God puts in His people. Discover your divine purpose then stay right on track. We were not designed to do everything by ourselves but just work as our heads need shoulders and our legs need feet, so we should work as members of the same body with Christ as the head.

THE POWER OF DREAMS

It is said dreams are the pinnacle of all men, where the mountains and valleys are moved by the flick of a finger, where the dragons and the fire exhaling monsters are dispersed at the word of the mind. Dreams are in every sense a level of life where everything impossible in this life turns into the possible. Joseph's brothers knew the reality and power of his dreams. Even his father could not accept his dreams yet truth had its footprints sinking search in the dreams of the young Joseph.

Every suffering person has to know that dreams are a recipe for things to come. They spice up the menu of a breakthrough and without dreams (expectation); timing becomes only a pinch of seasoning in an uncooked pot of farinose puree. Dreams are a touch with the reality not seen; it is in them that we find the evidence for things not seen and the substance for things hoped for. With them we grow our faith and as the Bible proclaims 'Without faith it is impossible to please God'. We all need dreams, be it we are suffering or not we all need them. They push us hard along the grains of time. Have dreams! Get prepared to receive through dreams for in them opportunities are realised.

OPPORTUNITY

Opportunity always has to meet preparation otherwise God will not redeem you from your pain. Be prepared to receive a breakthrough first and then ask the Lord for it. If you believe it then you can receive it. If you can see it then you can have it, for the word proclaims "whatever you ask for in my name believe that you have it and you shall receive". The moment Joseph understood God was still in speaking terms with him even in the dirty quarters of a derelict prison in the litter dumping areas of Egypt, it did not take him a whole decade to receive his way out of jail and move in to the flamboyant foyers of Pharaoh's palace.

By opportunity spotting and fulfilling other people's dreams first I am not at all condoning the con man tele-evangelists who only tell you to send money to their ministries so you can receive blessings. Some proclaim to be prophets and prophetesses yet they did not prophesy anything and still do not. Whilst there is nothing wrong in helping other people spread the gospel, there has been a devastating problem in that some of them (only some and not all) restrict the blessings being given to the sufferer by God as a result of the sending of money to their ministry only. That is a grave miscalculation that shows all the signs of illegitimacy and con-man-ship.

My Bible confirms that helping the poor, the fatherless, the sinners and the alien e.t.c wherever they are will always cover a multitude of sins, tap into the blessings of God and by it we receive our breakthrough. It is not only by sending our hard earned money to some confused tele/street-evangelist and after we do not receive this breakthrough start to blame God. God is always there to help but His people as He says are dying because of lack of knowledge. Joseph helped unrepentant people in jail by interpreting their dreams only and not by giving them money (again there is nothing bad about material help but be careful). Do not let any mortal fool you, God of heaven and earth, the mighty God himself is not after your substance but after your lack.

Again, Joseph's denial of ego was not shown by his financial help to others but just the interpretation of dreams. Be prepared to help others in your exploits so as to meet your opportunity. If you have a conviction that supporting someone's ministry is your call then do it with your entire mind but be very sure to survey the ground where you sow your seed for the degree of your harvest is in part determined by the fertility or infertility of the ground. You have a call to fulfil other people's dreams first before yours. Practise it and you shall receive your breakthrough by the will of God. Even if it is hard to bear when God says it, no man should tell you otherwise but be wise as serpents and peaceful as doves. If it becomes hard, just bear in your mind that God's strength is increased in your weakness and He will fight your wars for you. It is His word and He will wait upon it to perform it.

Never lose heart, your redeemer lives! But we should all conquer so as to go past conquering it is a divine law:

> "...when your endurance is fully developed, you will be...ready for anything" [James 1:4 NLT]

CHAPTER FIVE

MEETING THE REAL YOU IN THE MIDST OF GOD'S SILENCE

> "The fire of the Lord fell, and consumed... the wood and the stones, and the dust, and licked up water that was in the trench...and he (Elijah) took them (Baal's four hundred and fifty prophets) and slew them there...and when he (heard Jezebel was coming) he arose, and ran for his life..." [1 Kings 18 vs. 38, 40 and 19 vs. 3]

Through the identity parade the thraldom of silence wax into an abnormal normality that exposes and purifies the ultra mundane spirit in our inner beings. Synonymous with a candid, it seeks out the deepest things of our lives even without the best of our apprehension, exhuming and dumping the null and void moiety of our lives leaving us with a heart that requires more of the lord. This suffering phase is the lord's call that in every point keeps us in touch with our everyday limitations. The mortal flesh with all its stature if kept away from its real identity weaves an alien idea that it is either here by accident or it is on this world as an immortal soul; a kind of spirit having an unending natural experience if you get the lingua franca.

My craving as an author and a message bearer apart from dictating revelation is to efface every sufferer to life's blared echo where the utter existence of our identity hover above us, marred by a rollercoaster of pain and emotions that have taken us on a diabolic journey, side longs, over, in and out of our divine intuition; THE IDENTITY PARADE:

> "When he saw that he arose and ran for his life…" [1 Kings 19 vs. 3]

Embedded in the very core of Elijah, waiting for him in the pits of his being is his real 'self'. His primary exigency like any sufferer reading this book is never to run for his life but to extend a hand and be acquainted with the spirit man inside. Even if he is to let go of his current pained 'self'- will he be bold enough to stand in akimbo before the real Elijah who slew more than four hundred of Baal's prophets?

It is just a battlefield of the mind that needs to be fought sometimes .In this painful path of pain we need to understand that there is a place were we need to evaluate ourselves and see who we are in Christ before we continue in pain. Without this analysis we are bound to remain under pain's chains.

The whole idea lies not in comparing our suffering or the depth of our scars to our ability but in comparing the greatness of our God to the impulse of the problem or predicament being experienced. This however can not be experienced before we realise who we really are in Christ first and what Christ did for us in the past and continues to do both in the present and the future. Elijah has just been used as a point of contact to slay more than four hundred prophets of Baal but before we know it, he is already running away from Jezebel, running away in fear for his life. If his real 'self' would approach him will he be able to answer?

"Have we met before?", the running Elijah might ask "May be", the Elijah who slew Baal's prophets responds "I have so much respect and adoration for you that I wish I were you...not running from this woman Jezebel as I am doing...", says the running Elijah.

"You are really me but you have just forgotten and as a matter of fact you listened to your flesh instead...if you become me you won't run away from this pagan", the real Elijah who slew the prophets of Baal seems to respond.

The spheres of identity parade are a profound mist and an unfathomable stupor to any sufferer whether at the end of the spectrum or near for in it is laid another point of how and why God allows suffering and pain. The moment you realise the real you then you will know he that is in you is greater than the degree of predicament being suffered. Remember it is no longer you that lives but Christ that lives in you so if he lives in you then His unquestioned authority over principalities and powers also takes habitat in you counterbalancing and effacing every catastrophic situation and circumstance you might face or might be facing. This identity recognition is to any mortal a definite pre-requisite of faith. It is in itself a concrete pillar for faith to build up.

No faith can be experienced without you understanding your rights and place in Christ and without faith it is not only difficult but my Bible proclaims 'without faith it is IMPOSSIBLE to please God.'

Without the predominance of identity realisation we become more than serfs of pain, nimbly relinquishing who we really are in Christ and in no time fortifying even the frailty of our finite minds. We become brave against God and if truth be told coward against man, running away from pain and suffering when the power of God to move us out of our situation is starring us in the face waiting to be tapped in to.

Dungeons of mal faith effectuate an identity epidemic that latently circumscribes the extent of God's power- in every way expelling the hand of the God who redeems. Elijah's failure to recognise and understand God's intonation causes him to run away from Jezebel- a godless pagan woman just after he had called fire to come down from heaven. Without this identity parade spot on we become empty quivers on a fighter's armour; equipped in significance but lacking an antidote: arrows.

Life to Elijah became glory alloyed with a dish of pain, suffering, silence and scorn. God to him had hung up at the other end of the line and the heavens as he knew them had become nothing more than a bundle of engaged party lines. He (God) was silent. Neither logos nor rhema could be viewed within the boundary lines of his adversity. Neither the ooze of the future promises of God nor the memoirs of the yester-hours' victory over more than four hundred prophets of Baal gave him succour. This normal situation occurs and recurs to sufferers who easily in the midst of troubling situations lose their identity in Christ. It encroaches on them, preys on their inner being that they forget who they are in Christ and by so doing deny unawares the ability of Christ to turn right the bad circumstances right about them.

THE LACK OF IDENTITY

It is a reality of pain to take hold of a sufferer's identity. The cripple at the pool of Bethsaida was not mentioned by name, the word simply referred to him as a cripple. The woman with an issue of blood was in no way mentioned by name. Only her condition is known; twelve years with her sickness. Pain if not charily appreciated will capture our identity and our circumstances become the identity.

What differs from many of us who suffer is, unlike the woman and the cripple with an issue of blood they came to a place where they said this suffering had to end. They had a burning hope to find that breakthrough and when the catalyst came they were in a place to receive. They positioned themselves for glory.

Your enemies though agreeing in little, they will differ in many important issues of life concerning who you really are. The question Jesus asked His disciples was, "who do people say I am...", and the disciples stated their answer with; "some say..." Even among your colleagues there might only be one who understands you. If you take a panoramic view on the follow up scriptures only Peter said the correct thing, all the eleven seemed to be dumbfounded. The case however is not with Peter but with the eleven who kept quiet. Many people who misunderstand you are the friends you thought had a revelation on your identity and only one can understand you. Look for them.

THE POWER OF AN ANOINTED FRIEND OR FATHER

Find the one who understands you, exhort each other, look for the spark, that spark that made them know your identity and tell them you are the rock.

Samuel found Eli and Elisha found Elijah. When Elisha found his spiritual father the scriptures say he left everything he was doing and followed the man he believed had a powerful and evident anointing. It does not matter how they present themselves. If they have a word for you from God then capitalise on it.

Eli himself, if you look at the scripture was a fat man, suffering from obesity but God used him anyway which is a representation that God will sometimes bring you a word using an unlikely vessel. He can bring you a word through someone you think lowly of. That is what God is like. It is then up to you to deny or receive and embrace the word that gives you a breakthrough whether you hate the message bearer or not. My advice to you beloved is search for your Eli or your Elijah. Take heed of the word they have for you and if it is proven to be from God then your breakthrough might be nearer than you sense.

GOD'S UNCONDITIONAL LOVE: THE IRONY

> "and behold there was a cake baken on coals and a cruse of water above his head..."
> [1 Kings 19 vs. 6]

Forty days and forty nights, Elijah drifted through the wilderness, the sprite of fear far from ebbing. Meanwhile, God manifested his power, love and presence in the midst of a silence that up to now had seemed an eternity. He delegated His angels to minister to Elijah's necessities; even cakes were baked for him. The vogue which God uses in the evacuation; baking cakes, offering him water to drink, all this hospitality from Mount Carmel to mount Horeb assumes and weaves a latent vacuole in the enigma of pain and the mystery of suffering..

This true biblical story of Elijah exhibits that God sometimes, somewhere, somehow protects us through our adventures just the way we want them to go, though He might not even have ordained it. We, because of lack of stable identity always assume that God has ordained it but the shocking news is He will have not have assigned it to the extent that when we reach our destiny at mount Horeb he stands at the finishing line and utters the virtue draining question;

> "Why are you here...Go back the way you came..." [1 Kings 19 vs. 13, 15]

What? Wait a minute. Are you saying what I am contemplating you said? Are you the selfsame God who brought me all the way through the fearsome jungles to this location and baked cakes for me on the way? Yes, He did but did not commission it; He only gave Elijah food and watched over him because of His abundant mercy and agape love. What Elijah had was only God's said word (logos) and not His (rhema) the saying word. In other words many sufferers by failing to realise their identity lose the ears to discern God's voice so what they only have is the 'how to' instead of the 'do it now'. They do not make the grade in the realisation of God's saying word. In other words what these suffering believers have is the noun and not the verb, the logos and not the rhema.

RHEMA AND LOGOS

Eve would just be a wonted rib buried deep down in the diaphragm of Adam, and Adam a lump of ground loam with no life or voicefication, and the earth formless if there was no rhema. It is this rhema- the saying word of God that yields the enacting power and not the logos. Rhema in a nutshell is the Holy Spirit quickening the logos to manifest a miracle. Elijah occluded his mind to the sound of rhema, clinched the logos and ran away from Jezebel instead of subjugating her just as he had done to the prophets of Baal.

All that was in Elijah was the logos- God's said word and not God's saying word (rhema). Every believer has to respite for rhema before moving an inch for without this great move of God, it becomes extremely implausible to harvest spiritual fruits, surmount the evil of pain and that will give ancestry to an Elijah mentality; bolting away instead of confronting the adversary.

It is with this same rhema that the waters of the red sea were parted, the universe came into being, the seas are kept within their boundaries, the mountain goat gives birth, the snow hoses down and everything visible or invisible came into existence. Elijah ignored the very significance of this important point of faith, its power, significance and reverence. He dislodged that beyond perfect power that moves mountains and enshrines the heart of Christ; he simply arrived before departing. Many a time we clasp on to the logos but God's silence perpetuates to serve us with unrelenting serfdom if we become heedless of God's saying word- *rhema*.

God's saying word, grace and love is His essence. If Elijah had waited for God to speak he would have beyond even-handed doubt remained at Mount Carmel. Rhema gives you a sure word of the exploit God expects you to undertake. Christ Himself uttered this rhema all the time in his performing of miracles. There were always words like, 'come' 'E-ph-pha-ta', 'be healed', 'be made whole' are just some of the rhema emitted by Christ to everyone who wanted God's healing power to flow through their failing bodies. He used the word 'come' to Peter when he wanted to toddle on water. Peter understood that if God was not going to place rhema in his predicament then an abortion of the exploit would be imminent.

> "Lord, if it is thou, bid me to come unto thee on the water...and He (Jesus) said 'Come'...Peter walked on the water" [Mathew 14 vs. 28-29]

The lord told me that 'people often suffer because they fail to hear my voice; instead they assume I said something I never said'. Sometimes we all wait for possessions we already possess, we ask God unendingly, begging and pleading when all God wants us to do is appreciate him for the things that He has already given us (those things we ask for without knowing that we already possess). Quit begging for what you already own. Anyone can feel, so do not limit yourself to feeling the presence of God around you but strive to really know and hear beyond depth and beyond height when God speaks His rhema to you. Obedience to the saying word of God is the guarantee of dynastic continuance and the blessings of the Almighty God. Don't make a move before He says go; stay put until you hear His saying word. It is very adorable to talk the word but even more endearing to get the word to speak to you and when the word does speak to you there should be an exigency to get a revelation towards your healing. See, it is rare to get a breakthrough through someone's revelation though easy to get it through someone's anointing (hope you understand the knack).

Rhema should be real to you as a believer. Do not always get another person to hear your rhema for you, God never meant you to solely rely on the hearing ears of others in this new covenant. Get a hunger to hear not only God's said word but God's saying word – *rhema*.

THE GREAT ANALOGY

David Yonggii Cho a spiritual friend and the founder of the largest church in the world gave a very inspired explanation to the events that the Christian church witnessed in Korea with regards to rhema, which is the saying word of God: I quote:

Once in Korea a preacher by the name Yun Hae Kyung had a tremendous youth meeting on Samgak Mountain... people came forward, they would fall down, slain under the Holy Spirit. Many young people would flock to the meetings...During the week of the youth campaign it rained heavily, and all the rivers overflowed. A group of young people wanted to go to the town on the opposite side of the river, where the meetings were being held. But when they came to the bank of the river, it was flooded. There was not a bridge or boat to be seen, and most of them became discouraged.

But three girls got together and said, "Why can't we just wade through the water? Peter walked on the water, and Peter's God is our God, Peter's Jesus is our Jesus, and Peter's faith is our faith. Peter believed, and we should do all the more. We are going to go over this river!"

The river was completely flooded, but these three girls knelt down and held their hands together, quoting the scriptures containing the story of Peter walking on the water, and they claimed they could believe in the same way. There, in the sight of the rest of the group, they shouted and began to wade through the water.

Immediately they were swept away by an angry flood, and after three days their dead bodies were found in the open sea...

This became a topic of discussion all over Korea, and many previously good Christians lost their faith. They would say "These girls believed exactly as our ministers taught; they exercised their faith. From the platform our pastors constantly urge the people to boldly exercise their faith in the word of God. These girls did just that, so why didn't God answer? Jehovah God must not be a living God. This must just be a formalistic religion we have been involved in"

What kind of answer would you give to these people? Those girls had believed. They had exercised faith based on the word of God.

But God had no reason to support their faith. Peter never walked on the water because of Logos, which gives general knowledge about God. Peter required that Christ give a specific word to him: Peter asked, "Lord, if you are Jesus, command me to come"

Jesus replied, "Come"

The word Christ gave to peter was not Logos, but rhema. He gave a specific word "Come" to a specific person, Peter, in a specific situation, a storm.

Rhema brings faith. Faith comes by hearing, and hearing by rhema. Peter never walked on the water by knowledge of God alone. Peter had rhema.

But these girls had only logos, a general knowledge of God, and in this case, the working of God through Peter. They exercised their human faith on logos: that was their mistake. God, therefore, had no responsibility to support their faith and the way these girls exercised faith and the way Peter exercised faith is as the difference between night and day" **I close the quote**.

In light with the knowledge and lesson in this analogy we are bound by the wisdom of God to analyse every situation before we try and go on with our exploits. If God does not give a definite word for a definite situation let us wait and enquire of Him who gives wisdom in abundance to those who ask of it. It is always humanity's mistake to speak where the word in all its inerrant and sufficient state is silent and at times to antagonise what the word of God has to say.

Always wait for the rhema, the saying word of God for in it is all the victory. God has to say something to you first before you embark on whatever you set out to do for the Kingdom. It is very possible that often sufferers and those enjoying life skip God's rhema due to the fact that they try to psychoanalyse God, put him on an operational table, dissect Him to their own desecration and come up with immature and diabolic post operation report. Once they do this it spins them from being believers into just mere analysts, double minded, worldly pundits who will not receive anything from God for the scriptures still maintain that a double minded person will never receive anything from God. Wait for God's rhema.

GOD NEVER STARTS UNTIL ITS LATE!

"...turn thee eastward, and hide thyself by
the brook Cherish that is before Jordan..."
[1 Kings 17 vs. 3]

God's solution births a series of adieus to hope, erects as it were rubbles in the brain and places a flood of embraces to pain. Elijah's state of mind is left with very little to desire and a lot to fear. The God he was used to has become again, an intangible entity far gone from the environs of his suffering. His judgement of the situation is a mere lottery, he gambles with uncertainty, the certainty of conquering is no where near him, he is waning; everything around his being has deadened but to God Cherish is not the end. It is not even the beginning. The satire still lingers; Cherish means drought. It is a place oozing with futility and hunger. Elijah is dislodged from the clutches of Ahab's sword after the contest at Mt Carmel and ushered into the loins of drought. Better:

"I have commanded the ravens to feed you"
[I kings 17 vs. 4]

Just the citation of "feed you" must have demolished the negative attitude of Elijah but God's jelly-kneeing series was far from denouement. It seems He has employed pain more than is necessary (at the weighing of my mind that is);

"...the brook dried up..." [I king 17 vs. 7]

Again God appears silent but in the thick of that deafening silence He spoke other words that are full of bile.

"Go to Zarephath of Zedon..."

The whole situation of Elijah from Ahab to Cherish, from Cherish to Zarephath now comes as an auspicious of chimeras to the suffering mind. In all understanding it is not the way that God uses but the seemingly senselessness of it that creeps on a sufferer. Zarephath itself means smouldering furnace. What is God trying to do with Elijah's now miserable life? What if He leaves him on his own? What will happen to him? He has turned Elijah's life inside out and now Elijah is making the transition from the frying pan into the crimson hot fire. Elijah is juxtaposing with the blasting furnace, coiling in the unseen hope of an unseen God, waiting for a seemingly far breakthrough and most importantly swimming in the very thought of imminent melancholy. Death seems nigh but is God finished with him? No, no! God has just begun...many a time it is His divine law never to start until it's too late.

To Elijah, like many of the suffering souls, existence remains a mean and lamentable experience. It is just but nostalgia of a couple of yester-year smiles. He is in anguish but God provides antidotes to every pain. The drying up of the brook represents a time when a sufferer is marred by immense catastrophes but Zarephath which seems to be a further furnace stands for God's 'confusing' ways of meeting our need. It all lies in the sense that when the going gets tough the tough is nearing depletion.

It evokes a sense in the intellectual minds that God can send you to some seemingly foolish place to get your breakthrough and like Elijah we have to succumb to God's orders for He is the only redeemer with a definite word. In Elijah's predicament in Cherish we are shown how God meets a need but what is in Zarephath that we may smile about? What can God give that we as sufferers can understand?

> "...I have commanded a widow to sustain thee..." [1 Kings 17 vs. 9]

Elijah is driven into a place where his only belief centres on being really sustained by God, he is hungry, thirsty and he reaches for hope that his redeemer will vindicate him and be on His side and all God says is 'a widow will sustain thee'. Are there no rich people in Zarephath who are in good books with Elijah's God and our God? If there are then why should Elijah get sustenance from a widow? The Great God Jehovah who created millions of galaxies, milk ways, holes, planets and all could not give another option to Elijah's point of sustenance except; A hungry widow with a dying son. Wow! Wow!

God will always draw us nearer to our breakthrough by offering solutions He Himself knows are the best to be employed in that situation. It does not really matter whether we understand, appreciate them or not, God will employ them anyway. Let it dawn in your mind and heart that God is His own interpreter, He will make it plain if you dare listen and occlude to His will for your life through your suffering.

THE LAW OF LIMITATION

It must be known that everything God does will always keep you in touch with your limitations. He will never leave you to wholly think of yourself as the bread and butter of your own life that is why it is said the hardest time for an atheist is on the death bed when their minds run in the pursuit of a redeeming God. The laws of limitations are a regulator God uses on His creation so as to eradicate the sin of PRIDE.

At one point Elijah says he was the only prophet left but God denies his claim. He informs him that He has reserved seven thousand men to serve him.

Remember how great Elijah was; he was there at the transfiguration, the guy really went to heaven by a whirlwind, his spirit was commanded by God to come back in the person of John the forerunner. He was just great that you would think he knew everything yet God proves to him that he still has limitations. It is God's law of limitations that humbles mortals like you and me. We are always kept in touch with our limitation by the path of pain and suffering. Above all agencies pain and suffering are the most powerful systems to keep humanity in touch with limitations and call on a Mighty God.

God's "series" turns Elijah from living under an order that only breeds habit but makes suffering breeds life in its abundance for his servant, Elijah. No matter how ironic this journey Elijah undertook seems, God was neither silent nor intangible. He was always there and in it He exposes the will and the power to give us something more valuable even if it seems oblique to our carnal minds. He will show up unexpectedly in the middle of that need we have been desperately craving for all along.

> "…a handful of meal in a barrel" [1Kings 17 vs. 12]

It seems absurd and very little doesn't it? Where would a handful of meal in a barrel take the widow, her son and Elijah for that matter? The reality of realities is we can only espy a euphonious sufficiency a "handful of meal in a barrel" can be by working our potential through Jesus Christ, the great I AM who strengthens us, the author and finisher of our faith, the Alpha and the Omega.

> "Fear not… for…the barrel of meal shall not waste, neither shall the cruse of oil" [1 Kings 17 vs. 13, 14]

God never starts until it's too late. When your spouse is packing the backs and ready to leave you, that is when He starts. When the land lord is knocking at the door with an eviction order that is when He starts. When you are bed ridden in a certain hospital somewhere, that is when God starts. When your circumstances seem irreversible that is when...See! He always starts when the things you took for granted are dwindling or have dwindled. Come to think of it ravens are the extremely stingy animal you can ever find on earth yet God uses a raven to feed Elijah. You might smile at this but this bird is also one of the filthiest animals- in fact the Israelites regarded it as unclean. God can use all the unlikely sources to bring a breakthrough. Wait upon Him even if the only thing between you and poverty is nothing more than a handful of meal in a barrel and a little oil in a cruse.

When we feel he has forgotten us He brings a breakthrough. He might not show up when we want him to but He is always there on time.

CHAPTER SIX

DISMOUNTING THE ROLLERCOASTER OF PAIN

"...I have not a cake, but a handful of meal in a barrel and a little oil in a cruse: and behold, I am gathering two sticks that I may go in and dress it for me and my son THAT WE MAY EAT AND DIE [1 Kings 17 vs.12]

The widow's life pages open and close before her weary eyes. She is treading in arenas no man has treaded before. Not only is she depressed and disappointed, she is also a single mother. Not only is she a widow, she is a hungry single mother. Not only is she a hungry single mother, she also has a hungry son. Not only is the son hungry, he is dying.

Between her and poverty is one bucket of barley and a single cruse of oil. She and her son are at loggerheads with death. It is neither her disappointment nor the widow's ignoranceo-factata of not trying to face life beyond lunch that threatens my conscience, the most annoying and burdening punch line of her predicament becomes a sword of flame boiling and stirring my blood as a carrier of this message because more than everything I have said about the widow's suffering there is a clear-cut chafe: she is a GODLY WOMAN!

I am not going to dissipate the pages of this volume arguing the regards of the widow's 'help' voicifications to God, firstly, because the scriptures are reticent about her actual prayers and secondly her prayers have nothing to do with this final chapter in her miserable life. What we desire to be acquainted with is: If she was a GODLY PERSON- why did she suffer?

> "I am gathering two sticks that I may go in and dress it for me and my son that we may EAT AND DIE."

Submerged in that widow's aging frame are cries of a little girl, an adolescent, concealed far away from the real and tangible world. The toddler in her cries to be exhumed yet for a long time; she had drowned into a grotesque dirge to conceal the shadows of non vocal and useless feminine biceps. Her attempt to hoodwink us to the reality of the insecure little girl inside her makes her a hazard to herself. Only her creator can exhume the chaff and provide a prescription. God prescribes a dose of pain instead. Only this can exhume the dirty toddler within her.

A DOSE OF PAIN ANALYSED

God's silence in the midst of adversity takes another ugly phase. It causes the level of the widow's emotions to ascend leaving her with a void physical and spiritual belly that is ready to swallow anything of the spirit. This is by all means an attempt to get sufferers like you and I to a place were we can find a fresh ground to put into effect the freedom of choice already imbedded in us by God.

Disappointed by God

Underneath the widow's inner being, the horn of salvation sounds but she can not hear or understand the melodies thereof; she is already full of a diabolical zeal to deny her creator (a stance normally assumed by all sufferers at one point or another). The widow looks at Elijah and spits a ricochet of unbelief.

"...As the LORD THY GOD liveth, I have not a cake..." [1 Kings 17 vs. 12]

The declaration "as the Lord thy God liveth" shows an absolute denial of any affiliation with God. Hunger has transformed a Godly woman into the devil's vessel. She is seeing God as Elijah's, not hers. She is stuck and deprived in a rut – with no immortal or mortal to turn to except her estranged self. Slowly she is slipping into a deep hole caused by a life that has been pulverised by kinky demons masquerading as heavenly hosts.

The diagnosis is never a far-fetched; a closer appraisal of what she has been entertaining in her ex-Godly mind shows too many calories of insecurity, indecision, unbelief and a fruitless hope for nothing good.

"...and we may eat and die"

Even if death has blossomed as the new lieutenant of a certain canton, with hunger topping polls as the best newcomers on Lucifer's sin crammed bill boards. It still does not mean that God has vanished. He is in close quarters in our problems, even closer to us than we are to ourselves, more than willing to give us a hand if we only dare to believe.

In the filing cabinets of this widow's soul are robes of choking uncertainties. She has rented wedding rings from realms of unbelief causing her to hastily forgo that when educators teach mankind, they do it with charts and chalkboards but when Jesus teaches us He uses storms and adversities.

To the widow this is the end but to God it is only the beginning of the very end. A very happy ending for God never starts until it is too late. There was no light and God said 'let there be light'. There was no firmament and God said 'let there be a firmament'. He never starts until it seems like all hope is gone. There was no oil and no meal but God said:

> "The barrel of meal shall not waste, neither shall the cruse of oil fail..." [1 Kings 17 vs. 14]

I am convinced beyond depth and height that mankind constructs a great sense of intellectual moulding both in the breakthrough and in ages of turmoil. Just as theory comes from experiment, so is a breakthrough from turmoil through the grace of God. The reality of suffering on earth is like what life and death and virtue and vice are – they cannot exist without being qualified by their opposite.

When Adam and Eve fell they constructed a natural law of pain which God can only oppose as an act of benevolence and not as a must. Neither is He obliged to oppose it nor can he be forced to answer for it.

> "Wherefore, as by one man sin entered into the world, and death (everything bad) by sin; and so death passed upon all men, for that all have sinned ... [Romans 5 vs. 12, bracketing: mine]

I prefer sullen facts to analysing the complexity of uncertainty. The reality of suffering surrounded by the fall of mankind will always be a boil in the armpits of many mortals. Neither bulldozers nor evangelical ethics can destroy the catastrophes accommodated by the word of God for, "by one man sin entered into the world, and death..." It is with this truth that we accept an uncertain world full of uncertainties yet replete with Christ's agape.

The clear factor that there is a natural law set by us (Adam and Eve) should begin to tinkle in our minds and lead people to the only antidote- Christ.

The widow however, was under a bushel that ingrained her mind. She failed to see beyond a cruse of oil and a handful of barley. She thought of God as an unmovable god of Greek philosophy or an angry Allah of Islam who punishes and never feels remorse. Behind the widow's mask, God spoke and the end became the beginning. When she had nothing to hope for God gave her hope. He never starts until it is too late! If you feel you are drowning in seas of depression, He is there to start with drying up the waters of your calamities.

GOD HAS A WAY

It may seem extreme for you to think of how God will meet your needs but the reality remains, He created everything seen or unseen, He knows the end from the beginning- He knows His modes operandi, just dare to believe. Too many a time, we pray without hoping for an answer yet this grieves the Spirit of the most High God. If only you knew how God works: He is ready to deliver before we even think of saying our prayers. However our positive actions open the windows of Heaven but still other appalling ones close them- it is that simple. God is aware of our unbelief and is pained by it.

> "...is my hand shortened at all that it cannot redeem? or have I not power to deliver? Behold at my rebuke I dry up the sea, I make the rivers a wilderness: their fish stin-

keth, because there is no water and dieth for thirst. I clothe the heavens with blackness and I make sack clothe their covering" [Isaiah 50 vs. 2-3]

Though life might seem a tablet none can bear to swallow without gilding, I am pained by the words given to Isaiah by the Lord. The Lord is making a plea to the deafened ears of mankind. He gives an exhibit of his endless power yet we fail to apprehend His ability to break the yoke of calamities on our backs. It is a shame on mankind for our creator to be pained because there is no man on earth who is willing to receive what He has to offer yet He again says that 'eye has not seen, ear has not heard neither has it entered in to the hearts of men what God has prepared...'

We have folded our hands to His promises. We do not expect anything from Him though we are in need. We are sinking in a sin-filled pool with the iniquity of commission and iniquity of omission. We are right in the fields of remorse searching for sticks to chef our last meal so that we may get in and die. We are always commissioning what God did not commission and all the time omitting what He has commissioned. Isaiah chooses to be different; he is pained by his God's call for mankind to believe that He is an all-powerful God who is able to do greater and able to give in abundance above all that we can ever ask or think. Isaiah is in need and indeed ready to receive:

> "Behold the Lord God will help me; who is he that shall condemn me? Lo, they all shall wax old as a garment; the moth shall eat them up" [Isaiah 50 vs. 9]

Isaiah has received his refuge and for sure no-one shall condemn him. Is his God's hand shortened that He cannot deliver? No. does his God have power to deliver? Yes He does. Can He dry up the seas by rebuking them? Yes He can, even until the fish stinketh, because there is no water and they dieth for thirst [Isaiah 50 vs.2]. The widow should just trust!

THE RIDDLES OF GOD

Receive your miracle, God is waiting to deliver. He never starts until it's too late. When God started for the widow she had already felt the angel of death knocking at her door. I would have felt the same, I confess.

> "And it came to pass after these things that the son of the woman, the mistress of the house, fell sick; and his sickness was so sore, that there was no breath left in him…"
> [1 Kings 17 vs. 17]

The death of the widow's son emerges as one too many a catastrophe. Now, not only has she seen the angel of death, the angel has struck her son dead. The gong of a man of God sounds loud in her loins, she feels betrayed by Elijah, let alone by "Elijah's God". Her mind is wondering in the wilderness of loneliness, no one seems to care. Even her increased substance means nothing less than a bag replete with chaff.

The hope of a day turns to night and the sounds of joyful pianos turn to sorrowful melodies of a distant piccolo. The sunshine she was basking in turned to torrents of unstoppable showers. It is death, nothing less and she has no power to reverse the events. If she continues to cry would that help?

The God who increased her substance is nowhere near. The anguish she is in turns her to that little girl again, still buried inside her and mourning- the toddler inside her wants out! Widow or celibate, this is death, her son's death and it is painful. She cannot embody her pain. This is too much for her, more than it was when she expected to die. Her hopes were raised by Elijah's triumph but now the death of her only son takes her back to the real world, a world where pain rules the roost. She opens her mouth to pause a rhetoric question:

> "...what have I to do with thee, o thou man of God? art thou come unto me...to slay my son? [1 Kings 17 vs. 18]

WHAT TO DO WHEN YOU DON'T KNOW WHAT TO DO

It must be known in the very generic sense that the miracle surrounding increase in substance came after the woman's yielding to Elijah's demands. The prophet knows the widow is:

> "...gathering two sticks that (she) may go in and dress it for (herself) and her son, that (they) may eat and die" [1 Kings 17 vs. 12]

But is he not hungry enough to destruct every concentration of hope the widow had gained by seeing the man of God? Her intuition must have blossomed a day out of a cold and lonely night but Elijah wants more than the woman can anticipate.

> "...make me thereof a little cake...and bring it unto me" [1 Kings 17 vs. 13]

Can you hear the woman whimpering? Can you feel her pain? She is expecting an increase from the man of God yet Elijah has a decreasing plan. Not only does he feel hungry, he seems to forget the woman and her son are hungry, suffering and faced by uncertainty. His plan is not only a decreasing plan; it is a plan that defies all odds. He stops the woman from making a cake for her son and herself but instructs the woman to feed him first. Has he forgotten the woman is in a hurry to: "EAT AND DIE..."

> "...make me thereof a little cake first, and bring it unto me and after make for thee and for thy son" [1 Kings 17 vs. 13]

LORD! WILL YOUR DEMANDS STOP?

Though we cannot discuss the merits of her first prayers to God for help-it is evident the prayers are simply unanswered for she was preparing to die, but her prayer now contains an ingredient the first prayer never had, "giving". In lacking she baked a cake for the man of God and she received in abundance. God is always after a sufferer's lack and He will not trust you with His millions if you can not be trusted with your thousands. He can not be obliged to give you His healing if you can not be trusted with your pain.

> "The barrel of meal shall not waste, neither shall the cruse of oil fail" [1 Kings 17 vs.14]

We are challenged to be mindful of the rewards of giving (Whatever we have to give) in the midst of adversity when our eyes are sore with tears, when our days have turned into nights and when everything around has turned into a firestorm, for with God there is always a snowball even in the depth of hell and He is mightily moved in our weakness.

'GIVE ME', is Elijah's second request, he is still in controversial arenas of giving. The woman now knows the reality and rewards answering Elijah's request carry. For her it is never time to antagonise the man of God. She simply hands over her son, but the prophet's prayer needs profound connotations "hast thou also brought evil upon the widow...by slaying her son?" Is Elijah lost? Or has God brought evil upon the widow for foolery's sake?

God is still turning into the waves from the cries of useless masculinity in the widow's bosom. The widow HAS NOT LET GO OF THE TODDLER MENTALITY OF NOT CONFORMING TO PAIN. She is still concealing the child buried in her but God is not finished. In fact He will not finish until there are no signs of negative childhood within her.

In her mind, all that God has done by increasing her substance is just coincidence yet in reality coincidence is when God chooses to remain anonymous. She however receives her little boy back to life and she exposes that jelly-kneeing statement showing she really did not fully believe it was God at first. This is truly why God had allowed (not caused but allowed) pain to engulf her.

> "Now by this I know that thou art a man of God, and that the word of the LORD in thy mouth is truth" [1 Kings 17 vs. 24]

The principle of pain having the blue prints of all the helpful agencies in a sufferer's spiritual life is shed by the speech of the widow. Her mentality states an undeniable sign that a breakthrough draws a person to a rendezvous with God but this meeting however as with the widow's case comes heavily after suffering. It shows the fact that in pain we might not see God but in a breakthrough we surely can apprehend Him.

THE WIDOW'S DOMAIN

The principle of mixing giving and prayer is not necessarily a catalyst to show God is a demanding God, no! God is not. It is only because giving (whatever you give, be it faith or substance) represents a wave of humility and where there is humbleness in a believer pain escapes since God's Spirit is allowed to flow freely hence:

> "If my people who are called by my name shall humble themselves…I will…come down and heal…"

The widow decided to give in the midst of a problem and God moved in her predicament. Hannah in the book of Samuel vowed that if God would give her a son she would give the son back to God and God did. Samuel was born and became a prophet. She had to bargain with God for a breakthrough.

Jephtha after being faced with a desperate situation in a desperate army he had every propensity to use the strongest prayer he can find in the pages of his mind but this is what he chooses:

> "If thou (God) shalt without fail deliver the children of Ammon into mine hands, then it shall be, that whatever cometh forth of the doors of my house to meet me, when I return in peace from the children of Ammon shall surely be the Lord's…" [Judges 11 vs. 30, 31]

Jacob bargained with God by saying that if God would be with him and blesses him he was to give God a tenth of all and God answered Jacob's prayer by making him Israel, a nation. The lord Jesus Christ concurs "Salvation is from the Jews". Those are the majority of the Israelites for you.

Bargaining is a godly principle but we must without fail unmask every spirit that tells you to bargain with God by giving them your substance for many ravenous wolves have gone into the world as the word says. Be diligent and watchful when you are found with a calamity, bargaining might be your quickest way out but beware of wolves for I do not write this to feed them with an open ground to hunt their prey but I write to give the children of God a place to get their weaponry so as to fight their wars against the adversary.

A DELAY IS NOT A DENIAL

Sometimes God's delays can emerge to you as a denial. Our problem is we make up our minds that when God delays our answers He has denied. Sometimes He gives us what we really need instead of what we really think we need. The widow wanted food to survive, she wanted profit and what she got was a Prophet.

Do not be quick to lose heart let us just wait until our 'Samsons' touch the pillars of the coliseum. The Philistines took him to make sport of him but God was positioning him for the next great things of life. I understand that you might feel disappointed by God right now but I have a word for you - don't quit! What the enemy meant for bad, God has meant for good. What Delilah cut short while you were asleep, God is lengthening. The rumour that the 'Delilars' of this world took to your Philistines informing them you were asleep will definitely become a word of testimony that you are wide awake. It is only a matter of time. Though it may tarry, a time is coming when you shall shake the pillars of your calamity's habitat and the walls and roof shall destroy your calamity beneath you.

HOW TO KNOW IF PRAYERS ARE DELAYED OR REFUSED?

Scripture says 'let the grace of the lord be the rule' the word rule in Greek means umpire or referee that means if you as a surmounting sufferer abide within the shelter of the most High God then God will install an alarming device as it were so as to let you aware of the state of your prayers. This rule however is not tangible in the natural world but only in the spiritual and no one can say you do not have or you have for only you and your God can tell. Many sufferers who have a burning desire to overcome already posses this rule but the devil tries to fight their understanding of it and confuses them so that they may anticipate the worst instead of the best. The adversary will always try to confuse stress with bless because to him if they can rhyme then they can go together but when God blesses He adds no sorrow to it.

The enemy has always been trying and is trying to inject a dose of venom within your system, busy making diabolic suggestions within you. He knows if you can take it then he can overcome you. If you can think it then he will win the battle. Don't take it, refuse to offer the devil any chance to mess up with your life and always keep guard of thoughts by bringing every thought captive to Christ. Quit entertaining defeat in your life, always think big, and think 'OUT' of your calamity. Fight! Fight the good fight! [1Timothy 6 vs. 12]

God is ready to turn your mess into a message and your test into a testimony.

CHAPTER SEVEN

THE STUPIDITY OF FAITH

> "And Elisha sent a messenger unto him saying, Go and wash in Jordan seven times, and thy flesh shall come again to thee and thou shalt be clean" [2 Kings 5 vs. 10]

The ghostly glow of the Jordan River, with its muddy waters repelled Naaman. Even Elisha's sotto-voce confounded his lack of options and God Himself ignored Naaman's feel of seniority. The ghastly strike of thunder could not have pushed his ego. He was a suffering man full of pain from leprosy but he thought lowly of God's command. He became comfortable within his leprosy than in the remedy of washing himself clean in the muddy Jordan River. Why God did not choose the waters of Abana and Pharpa which were a lot cleaner troubled him:

> "Are not Abana and Pharpa rivers of Damascus better? than all the waters of Israel? May I not wash in them and be clean? So he turned and went away in a rage"

Namaan could not contain it. The word of God seemed to strip off him the shells of seniority complex long imbedded in him by the uncircumcised Syrians. Amidst this juncture of a gathering storm where the only hinge to his healing could be crushed by these dirty waters of Jordan, Namaan is torn apart and decides to leave. It is his idea that if God could heal him, the least he could do is do what to him seemed intellectual and that is bathing him in Abana and Pharpa, the cleaner rivers as compared to the suggested Jordan.

A difference of taste between an uncompromising, infinite God and a finite Captain became a monster gulf of strain. The infinite God is in heaven, clean, holy and alive, no leprosy in sight. Namaan, the captain is wondering in his weary world, his body swamped by leprosy. There is no one to help him with the exception of this man of God who keeps pointing his forefinger towards the muddy waters of Jordan. His servant though afraid of the disease lingers around with tremors in their voices convincing Namaan to occlude to Elisha.

> "Then went he down, and dipped himself seven times in Jordan, according to the saying of the man of God: and his flesh came again like unto the flesh of a little child and he was clean" [2 Kings 5 vs. 14]

THE FOOLISHNESS OF FAITH

Faith calls for that complete obedience to that which reason does not believe and in this, obedience is to belief what virtue is to vice. They again cannot exist without being qualified by their opposites. For in it, whatever God says is to be followed without a shadow of doubt or self suggested contra. This is a place where we cannot weigh the pros and cons of what God has instructed but where only the pros and the many illogical instructions are trusted so as to obtain the occurrences of the improbable

Many a time God's instructions sound, seem and are counted among the "foolish" things on this earth by those who have failed to unmask the power of the paradox. They have looked at the word of God, the dysfunctional areas of this world, the diseases and suffering on the earth and concluded that what God says is merely fiction- if not foolish.

They have seen God as a powerful entity but clad with a low intelligent quotient. You might say yes to that. Think of God instructing Moses to lift a handful of ground loam then turning it into mosquitoes. What of five loaves feeding thousands. What about a stick turning into a snake. Can I take you to Hosea being instructed to marry a prostitute just to fulfil God's own theological needs. Let us talk of Moses old as he was being instructed to raise a rod so as to give the Israelites victory in the war being fought in the valley.

What of Isaiah preaching naked for three years at God's command. Let us come back to the story of Namaan being told to wash his unclean leprosy in the unclean waters of the Jordan. You might agree with Namaan for surely what happened to the cleaner waters of Abana and Pharpa? Is there a bunch of holy quinine tablets within Jordan? No, but God just prefers the dirty waters to the cleaner ones. Hey!

God Himself shows no sign of concern or anger through all those ridiculous suggestions by His creatures. No wonder the Bible says:

> "...the foolishness of God is wiser than men;
> and the weakness of God stronger than men"
> [1 Corinthians 1 vs. 25]

GETTING TO GRIPS WITH STUPIDITY

That which seems to be stupidity to many is nothing less than God's uncompromising path to "...destroy the wisdom of the wise, and...bring to nothing the understanding of the prudent". The mantle of an infinite God's touch though looming shallow to the finite human mind, grooms and births the many helpful though seemingly impossible things of life, even pain and suffering we all go through irregardless of colour or creed. It is in these seemingly stupid commands of God that our destiny is shaped. God's main concern is to demolish the understanding of the prudent and blind those who say they can see. Paul asks:

> "Where is the wise? Where is the scribe? Where is the disputer of this world? Hath not God made foolish the wisdom of this world? For after that in the wisdom of God the world by wisdom knew not God, it pleased God by foolishness…to save them that believe" [1 Corinthians 1 vs. 20-21]

STUPIDITY OBSERVED

The problem of man is to propose what God disposes and by so doing erase the nigh future of a breakthrough which today's obedience purchases. In the midst of pain doctors and those close by offer diagnosis where God gives a prognosis of happy morrows. Many a time in these situations, instructions are unbearable and at most may prove to a human mind as if they are direct from the pits of hell.

As an author I do not only write to (as Mencken says) "attain that feeling of tension relieved and function achieved which a cow enjoys on giving milk", rather, I write to the suffering world as a command from God to dispel the many false prophets in this world who keep telling us of good times to come; where Daniel talks of pain and where Christ talks of:

> "Behold, I send you forth as lambs among wolves" [Luke 10 vs. 3]

By so doing these false preachers have preached as if we are still in the acceptable year of Christ when in actual fact we are riding the wings of Isaiah's virgin years. We are right in the hind legs of a kicking horse. It is important that we remember this for our eternal home is nearer to us now than it has ever been in the history of the body of Christ.

THE INTELLIGENCE WITHIN THE STUPIDITY

Though every being is entitled by the laws of this world to their own opinions, conclusions and confusions there is need to understand how God controls the mishaps of this journey called life. Even if one takes God to be an abstract entity that mitigates the woes of others the truth remains: God is inerrant and sufficient and His answers may come far from and short of the so-called intelligence of man. What we as sufferers or potential sufferers forget is life is a journey like any other journey. In it we will reach gradients, negotiate turns, round the corners and totter upon pot holes and if not careful get involved into immense accidents.

Namaan might have laughed out of his socks (if he had any that is) when the good news of his survival was delivered not only from a little girl but from a captive little girl. Couldn't God have found better people to deliver His word to the captain? To him it was a little bit insensible for God to talk through a small girl He (God) could not protect when they took her captive but God does what He sees best. Paul adds

> "For ye see your calling brethren, how that not wise men after the flesh, not many might, not many noble, are called: but God hath chosen the foolish things of the world to confound the...wise; and God hath chosen the weak things of the world to confound the

things which are mighty…" [1 Corinthians 1 vs. 26-27]

THE STUPIDITY OF VOTING

Paul talks boldly of the carnal mind being an enemy of God, "for it is not subject to the law of God". Christ concurs: "if you love me keep my commandment" [John 14 vs. 15].

Obedience to God's seemingly weird commands stems from a profound desire to understand God and embrace what I as an author has termed "the stupidity of faith" which is the ability to obey the seemingly stupid or "nincompoopish" looking commands of God, with the unmovable hope that all things will work together for those that follow God's commands. Imagine what it meant to Naaman with all his rankings in the Syrian army when the prophet of God sent his servant to deliver the message. Naaman might have wanted the prophet himself to talk to him but the prophet does not do that for some mysterious raison d'être.

Sometimes God will make you meet the least expected person who will offer you a crazy strategy to get your breakthrough at the time you may wish to speak to what every mortal calls the epitome of faith. Follow the commands, do not classify people or put them in to groups. Quit being God. The truth is God will demolish all of your predicaments if you quit begging for the power that you already have and stop voting on what He has already commanded you to do!

A certain story is again told of a mountain climber who slipped from the summit of Mount Everest only to hang in the air supported by his climbing rope. In his peril, the climber cried out to God for help: "Is there a God out there?" The climber cried out and the Lord was not silent that day so He answered the climber.

"I am here my son"

"Tell me what to do in my predicament Lord" the

climber begged.

"Let go of the rope that supports you" came God's response. Seeing and perceiving God's response as a hard nut to crack and an absolute impossibility the climber cried again in the gloom of the night.

"Is there another God out there with a different idea to that of the one who said 'let go of the rope'?" In the silent came another reply.

"My son there is no other God beside me and I am telling you again to let go of the rope before it is too late"

"Is there another option my Lord?"

"None my son, only let go of the rope and it will all be well. If you do not want to obey I am off, I do not have time for those who do not obey"

The climber refused to let go and as a result he was found dead the next morning by other climbers but surprisingly enough, *his corpse was just ten centimetres from the ground,* so when God said let go of the rope, He knew the distance the climber was from the ground would not kill him if he had let go.

There are many things in life that God tells us to take up, live or throw away and in many cases it would seem for a moment that His commands are vain and ill thought but we are called to follow them any way if we are to surmount the evil of pain. We should quit voting on what God tells us to do. Quit voting now and watch God do greater things in your life.

CHAPTER EIGHT

DEFENDING YOURSELF: THE ARMOUR OF GOD

Pain and anguish furrow my browse and turn my hair kinky, instead of journeying through life – I am dragged by it. On both shoulders the steel lining of my armour heaves an onus to my weary frame, blood oozing, eyes protruding, a shield is hanging on my right arm. I am poised to begin but just in case you think I am credulous, remember Apostle Paul informed me it really works for THIS IS REAL WAR!

> "Put on the whole armour of God, that ye may be able to stand against the whiles of the devil for we wrestle ..." [Ephesians 6 vs. 11-12]

Apostle Paul's "real war" synopsis looms hazy from where I am stationed. He preludes with dressing us up in seemly borrowed robes, assumes there is an imminent warfare ahead but in between the eulogy is laid a thesis well short of indispensable amendment. "Stand", is this armour literal? have I become a victim of Apostle Paul's self deprecating humour? Is there a real confrontation ahead? Is he well versed that history has it that "man" is just but a neutral bystander in the realms of suffering? What is he trying to do with this whole armour on me? First, he tells me this was war, I am ready to attack and he shifts tempo and says just "stand". Stand! Why? Can I succeed military action by standing? I feel ill omened. I am about to disarm myself but wait! There is still hope for a fight here. Apostle Paul is back with the reality of that war and the purpose of my shield.

> "Above all, taking the shield of faith, wherewith ye shall be able to quench all the fiery darts of the wicked" [Ephesians 6 vs.16]

The reality of this armour sparks controversy in the Christian ethics yet in the spiritual realm they are in a form of a physical shield and physical armour, tangible as it were. They deter darts of anguish, calamities catapulted by the adversary.

Even though I am close to battle, my loins girded with truth, the breastplate of righteousness, my feet shod with the preparation of the gospel of peace, the helmet of salvation and of course a gleaming sword of the Spirit which is the word of God. Before I go, I desire to gather the guarantees that my armour will not tolerate a single dart to touch my body. Apostle Paul comes to my rescue:

> "...ye shall be able to quench ALL the fiery darts of the wicked" [Ephesians 6 vs. 16]

Note that he says 'ALL' not just a few but all. I am ready now but wait! Why did Peter drown if the armour really works? why did the devil wrestle Peter to the extent of sinking? Why did his armour fail to detain ALL THE FIERY

DARTS as apostle Paul says. Is there the possibility that Apostle Paul is mendacious about the whole issue, is he being economical with the truth or He is a man trying to get a good word across on behalf of a helpless God?

WHY DID PETER DROWN IF HE HAD THE ARMOUR?

Peter's intuition failed to see beyond the storm. He camouflaged himself in a faith impaired gi, broke asunder the shield of faith and set limits for himself either to sink or be sunk- period. He is seen at the prologue, full of zeal the whole armour shining on him- oh! what a "Peter", he antagonizes the molecular density of water by walking on it. Its working, yes it should. Remember he is the only one who recognized Jesus walking on water. The other twelve attributed "walking on water" to a ghost, not Jesus, He couldn't do that! They were a little bit mad.

Peter was different, he knew Jesus was able and his faith therefore gave birth to the rigid armour. He walked for a while with his shield of faith right in front of him but BANG! He eradicated everything about God's rhema, chose to be flooded by manufactured instincts instead.

> "...but when he saw the wind boisterous, he was afraid; and beginning to sink, he cried..."
> [Matthew 14 vs. 30]

IT IS NOT EVEN THE HIGH TIDE THAT SANK Peter but the sight of it. His disembarking from faith and the spirit of fear overtook his faith, torn to pieces that shield and threw him in the abyss of the unheard of. By tolerating fear Peter contaminated his faith. Peter like many believers was entangled in the thorns of unbelief but though a fallen hero he is not forgotten. Jesus is waiting and at least He has seen Peter walk the hardest patches of his life.

We can walk on top of the waters (calamities) of our lives and in our prayers we should start to pray the answer and not the problem; pray the future and not the sinking because that is exactly how we should operate as amour clad believers, whether suffering or rejoicing. Fear can turn our faith into an unambiguous fret. It forms and transforms great faith into unbelief.

Bethmore says

> "If believers do not believe what on earth do they do?"

What a question! This piercing rhetoric question goes deep down into the heart of the problem. It stamps a seal that even elevates the scripture

> "Many shall have a form of Godliness but denying its power"

Peter eradicated praying the problem, he prayed the answer:

> "And Jesus reached out his hand and caught him…'…you of little faith why did you doubt'…" [Matt 14 vs. 31]

Whenever we lose that rhema and plummet to the floor, He is there. When we sink deep within the cares of this life He is there. When all hope is lost, He is there. When it seems near an end, He is there to begin. When it seems there is no one to hear our problems, He hears. When we are drowning and it seems to us there is no pillar to take us to safety, He holds out His hand and deeps down in to the water to rescue us. That is my God. We just need to reach into the depth of our inner person, feel the rhema and unlock the keys to the heart of God. Promptly we are reminded that in the nucleus of our lives is a formidable force larger than life, larger than anything we can visualize.

With unconditional love -agape, He fights our wars. If we only realise what omnipresent means we will always be able to see him and understand the mighty power our redeemer has. In what we believe were the storms that Peter dreaded, God was present seemingly still but all powerful. It is not God's will that humanity perishes but only that they endure both in suffering and pain for His love is not phileo (conditional), but agape (unconditional). He undergoes everything with us and within us and He is always:

> "...long suffering to us-ward, not willing that any would perish..." and He "...knoweth how to deliver...out of temptations..."
> [2 Peter 3 vs. 9 & 2 vs. 9]

God is not impressed by our self admiration or our so called strategies. He created our intelligence thus all the tricks in or not in the book He is well aware of. He knows how we think, act and react but He is there when we call. The prayer lines of heaven are neither engaged nor temporarily out of order that we can not reach or get in touch with our heavenly father. The almighty God Himself is calling to us in Psalms 91 vs15-16:

> "...call upon me, and I will answer...in trouble: I will deliver and honour...with long life will I satisfy, and shew...my salvation.

CALMING THE STORMS OF LIFE

> "And Jesus reached out His hand and caught him...little faith wherefore dist thou doubt...

and when they were come into the boat the wind ceased" [Matt 14 vs. 31, 32]

The irony of encountering and counterbalancing the storms of life is laid in the foundation that the turbulences of Peter didn't calm when Christ got hold of Peter's hand, they were still raging. Peter and Christ had to move against the storm yet they neither sank nor stumbled like Peter had done alone. (Read your Bible)

Peter managed to move through the midst of the storms with Jesus holding his hands. Only when they entered the boat did the storm cease. When we get out of the boat of those who do not believe and enter into the world of unrest we should concentrate on rhema, not forgetting the inhabitants of the boat who had only the logos, their burdens are lifted when they receive us with a testimony and the storms of their lives cease as a result of the word of our testimony. If we are to live within the truth of our lives we have to understand that we need to really get out of the boat and undertake the exploits set before us by Christ without taking in to consideration the wind's intensity or its mere look.

Remember when the same Peter was confined in prison, God broke his silence by freeing him and all those who were also bound with him. It is the principle of God's mercy to help those around you by the sheer answering of your prayers.

Sometimes what we define as silence is never God's definition of silence.

The silence of God other than being caused by pain as a helpful agent is at times, as the Psalmist says caused by:

"...your sins have hid His face from you that He will not hear" [Isaiah 59 vs. 2]

Peter's second attempt to oppose the molecular density

of water succeeded not because he had created vacuum feet or buoyant toes but because he had someone - not just "A somebody" but THE MAN. He had to renew His inner being, assume the stance he was in at first, wear the amour the Apostle Paul talks about and in its fullness faith always inhabit in us and without faith he would have sunk.

THE FACTS OF WAR

After all has been said and before all of us get excited about the impending war there is however the concept of fighting the devil which I wish to clearly reject and demolish from a sufferer's mind because the moment we as suffering Christians think of the devil as a foe to fight with, we miss it for the word says he was defeated at Calvary. We can never fight a foe that God Himself has already defeated. If we brew this doctrine it simply means we are saying God did not defeat him but by so saying we become liars. It should be noted that when apostle Paul talks about … he is not referring to fists flying and kicks kicking but as the Greek word wrestle means, he is simply referring to swerving meaning to make the devil lose course. No wonder apostle Paul says " STAND"

Our wars have already been fought what is left for us is to understand the greatest level of power we have by adorning ourselves in the armour of God and realise what the devil sees in that armour so as to be able to "resist the devil" as the scriptures consigns it.

CHAPTER NINE

ONE MORE DAY WITH THE TOADS

I invite you to the tip of my pen where these words (if not the revelation) are flowing from. Here is where the paradox becomes alive to your human eye, if not the spiritual. I promise to lead you through this ink to the problem of Pharaoh and Egypt. The problem among other things is that of FROGS, yes frogs. Can you see them? I can. They are the ones in Pharaoh's dish, they bath with him, eat from his plate. His supper has their odour. Do you smell them? Again I do. He opens his mouth to speak and that other glossy one leaps in. I ask you, do you really see them? I do. They are polluting Egypt. Their urine is a deadly contagion, the dead ones are strewn in his byways, highways and rot in his divan. I tell you I can see them. I am not the Pharaoh kind of mortal, if I am given the chance to get rid of these foul redolent creatures I would, there and then. Yes I would. You would too but the nincompoop Pharaoh did not. Here is his story, I promise to take you there. Yes there in the hub of Egypt. I really do, so I will.

"And Moses said unto Pharaoh Glory over me: when shall I entreat for thee, and for thy servants, and for thy people, to destroy the frogs from thee and thy houses, that they may remain in the river only? **And he ... (Pharaoh answered) tomorrow**" [Exodus 8 vs. 9-10]

Oh! What an idiotic emperor. He is choosing the **Morrow** instead of the **NOW**.

Many a sufferers are subjected by the dark recesses, the desperateness of their circumstances and the mere lack of optimism in their minds, to adopt a dire strand of the Pharaohic syndrome. Every fibre in Pharaoh opted for a better tomorrow free from frogs when he had the entire propensity to call off the toads right there, in that minute, hour and night, right in front of Moses and Aaron, there in that cold night. To him and to too many sufferers he could not fathom the depth of his problems being done away with in a split of a second, instead he thought of the frog dilemma being too life-size for even the God of Israel to settle within a twinkle of any Pharaoh's lazy ogle. But where is his kingdom Egypt in this verdict? Who is eavesdropping on her hungry and fading toddlers inside the city walls? Where is Egypt in Pharaoh's response?

Here she is crumbed in adversity: Egypt is swimming in a pool of toads, dead and alive are the smelling creatures yet the only man who has the aptitude to accept a breakthrough on her (Egypt) behalf has postponed it by a day, all with the sputter of his asinine mouth. The widows, the hungered poor, the homeless, the starving of this vast land of Egypt are sharing their habitat with unwanted guests, the frogs. The catch stands; it is pain's blue print many a time that even the rich share their plight with those at the bottom of the social, political and economic stratification. The reek of the frogs also crams their nostrils just as they stuff the nostrils of the 'always' unfortunate. When they die the same worm consumes them both, there are no golden worms to eat the flesh of the rich. They all mourn, yes, Egypt mourns yet her redemption is squeezed between Moses' question and their King's response; *Pharaoh's 'tomorrow'*. The question from Moses' lips is nothing closer to a confusing enquiry, it is just an undemanding question latently requiring the **'Now'** answer and not the *'Tomorrow'* response that the foolish Pharaoh thought of giving.

If you have forgotten the question then listen to Moses as he puts it to this Pharaoh:

> "*When shall I* entreat for thee, and for thy servants, and for thy people, to *destroy the frogs* from thee and thy houses, that they may remain in the river *only? And he ... (Pharaoh answered) tomorrow*" [Exodus 8 vs. 9-10]

A POINT OF REASON

There is also an immense fad within pain and that is to every so often try and identify with the decisive purpose for reason by an attempt to calculate or compute the chemical composition of a miracle. This need to Psychoanalyse God and put perimeters to the 'what and how' He can do what He says He will do crippled the Pharaoh of that day and still haunts the suffering Pharaohs of this day, you and I. Pharaoh's problem was not the answer *'tomorrow'* but the reason behind the answer. He belonged, was born and raised in a place where he worshiped the river gods of Egypt who never seemed to answer prayer except when the devil 'did' on their behalf. His tradition got in the way of his reason. Tradition like he never knew it dictated too well that a god will never give a quick response to the frogs of that magnitude except at throwing sticks that change into snakes. Whoosh!

He never acceded to the reality obtained by embarking on a journey to some place where reason sometimes seems nonexistent and where we realise other things can never be reasoned to be followed. When God gives an opportunity for removing our frogs form the palaces of our lives, we have to let God be God and leave him eradicate the problem before our very eyes be it we understand the when or how. Our exigency in answering to the 'when?' of God should be *'Now'* and not tomorrow. We are too blessed to be stressed, too stressed to postpone our joy even by a mere millisecond. By postponing our breakthrough even by a night like Pharaoh did we roam into the diabolic hubs of mal faith yet the word remains *"without faith it is impossible to please God"*

Hear this: The devil is just an unemployed cherub who is dead spiritually but worldly very alive and clever. He endeavours to control and manipulates what he hears us proclaim, adds thoughts to our minds and persuades the pained into accepting other things that they might not have thought possible under God's earth to accept. By his influence we hastily postpone our breakthrough. Sometimes this drastic postponement comes from getting surprised when God answers prayer rather than getting surprised when He does not. Got the knack? I wonder Reader if you are still at the centre of my biro?

God neither has a cherub studded parliament nor holy committees to debate and analyse prayer. Instead Isaiah the most learned prophet in the scriptures proclaims *"...it shall come to pass, that before they pray, I will answer ...while they are yet speaking, I will hear"* Pharaoh's notion of God is very contaminated. He is the kind of sufferer who prays with no clear hope that God will answer, [to him] whatever god that is, even his river god. He has no hope of Moses' God eradicating his rub pronto, for him tomorrow is more possible than 'Now'.

NOT ANOTHER NIGHT WITH THE FROGS

It requires an indomitable sufferer to understand the principle of taking action at the time the taking of the exploit is appropriate not when it has passed. Paul said 'I determined...' There is a moment in time when stuff gets straightened up by God and He gets ready to give you a breakthrough, this is a time to get our spiritual antennas up and wait for that question Pharaoh failed to answer "when do you want the frogs of your lives to depart?" we should by all means respond with a resounding 'right now' and not have a loan of the Pharaohic syndrome of crying out 'tomorrow' instead of today.

Reader, cry out 'Not another night with the frogs'. Change your perception of how and when God answers prayer and delve in to that secret place where you abide in the shelter of the most high God, *El Shaddai* himself not Pharaoh's *El sha- DEAD*. God can do it today for you. Stop listening to Pharaohic preachers who like the sound of He will do it on their lips and enquire into the He has already done it. Though it is not yet revealed in the natural, your breakthrough is in the lips of Moses, God has already delivered it both in the logos and in the rhema - His saying word.

Brethren, if you are too engrossed in your pain that believing what my biro just finished drooling becomes a hard nut to crack, I do not blame you (though you are to be blamed due to lack of faith) for I the message bearer could hardly contain this truth. It was hard for me to accept that the breakthrough that I yearned for all these years was already completed in the spiritual yet there was a need for me to bring it into the natural. Now I know, not another night with the frogs. Not another day with the toads. I refuse to eat with them, drink with them, bath with them, and sleep with them. I refuse to breath in their stench. I refuse. I am a peculiar person belonging to the holy priesthood. I am that person the Bible proclaims 'If God be with me no one can be against me'

Look at what Moses said in that foyer of Pharaoh's palace. He leans on the marble pillars of this vain beauty inhabited by this hoodwink. He utters:

> "**...that they may remain in the river only?** And he ... (Pharaoh answered) tomorrow" [Exodus 8 vs. 9-10]

In the Jewish idioms a river or water represents people or simply speaking the world. I do not know if you get the knack but if you do not here is the revelation; Moses' words of removing the frogs so that "...they remain in the rivers only..." show an undisputed word of where pain is 'intended' as it were, in the world of sinners since frogs in this case represent pain. It heralds a picture of past conquering and paradisiacal picture believers have to embrace in their journey through this natural experience we are having as spirits in flesh suites. Though we experience suffering as a result of what I have depicted in the previous chapters we have to get this in to our brains - suffering according to this analogy is rightfully for those not under the covering of God. Why do we have to suffer then even if the pain has God's blue print? Again I add an answer: because we exist in a world with sin and though we are spirits, let us not forget that we are having a natural experience in the same place where Adamic consequences of sin function in and out of the sons of disobedience.

Not another night with the frogs. Not another night with the toads. Not another night with my problem. Not another night with my circumstance.

CHAPTER TEN

THE POWER OF WHAT YOU ALREADY POSSESS

When trouble knocks at your door and you tell him there is nowhere for him to sit...he will tell you he has brought his own stool.
>> Chinua Achebe

You are not here on this planet to breath all our oxygen, spent all our living space, release all your carbon dioxide, eat all our food and cry a river till oceans flow. There drips in your inner being an ever full oasis of heaven's blue prints aimed at establishing an unconquered conqueror within you but without the realisation thereof, pain will play ball with your emotions, seize to be surmounted and grind you in to a lost scent inside a lily encircled by thorns and forgotten to the world. However, from the lone shielding of the might fog within us, the power of what we already possess define us and cry out to be exhumed. Only we can conceal them behind the shadows of our wrong mental state and the pages and diabolic mask of our profound lack of vision. Pain becomes a pain if we retain a sense of failing to realise the ability bestowed upon us before the abridgement of the human race.

> "Among all this people there were seven hundred chosen men left handed: every one could sling stones at an hair breath, and not miss" [Judges 20 vs. 16]

Among the Israelite army were seven hundred skilled men who could shoot a stone at hair's breath and not miss but they were so perplexed and frightened by the size of their problem (Goliath) that they cowered when they saw him, their knees buckled, their pants did not, their legs trembled before him and their stone quivers rattled with fear. The scriptures say these men literally ran in fear of this giant pagan yet David dared to be unique. He was pushed by a revelation far different from the rest of the Israelite army.

> "...David put his hand in his bag and took thence a stone, and slang it, and smote the Philistine in his forehead, that the stone sunk in his forehead; and fell, upon his face...so David prevailed over the Philistine with a sling and with a stone...and there was no sword in the hand of David..." [I Samuel 17 vs.49-50]

The gross miscalculation brewed by many theological 'pundits' and the so many non-theological ones (you and I) who profess that the stone David used to kill Goliath was Holy Ghost guided is a mere escape from the reality and a longest way of saying nothing and uttering the evidently unscriptural. It is in a sense a denial of that which God being God has imbedded within human beings, His creatures. David however exhibits that his knowledge for killing

Goliath came from his history in killing a lion and a bear. He simply says it was the practise that made him a victor. Although the practise was provided by God, David did not deny or hide the fact that God has a way of preparing His people for future events. As a measure to cut the long story short or the short story long David used what God gave him way before the time of his encounter with this uncircumcised Philistine by the name Goliath.

Your destiny lies in your ability to find what God has blessed you with, develop it through encounters with the lion and bears of pain, otherwise you will spend too much time praying and bothering God to give you what He has already given you. David knew the first time he had an encounter with the lion that it was God's fingerprint to what was to follow. Whilst it is the Holy Ghost of God that guides you, the reality is what that same Holy Spirit gives you will still remain within you even if you deviate from the way hence:

> "...gifts and callings of the Lord are without repentance..."

The Holy Spirit being God will not take away what He gave you but when you miss the point of contact then your gift stays dormant until you have in yourself a renewed person. One of the gifts David so much possessed was the ability and agility to move with the vision and to spot opportunities.

Have you ever researched on how the armour of the Philistines or the Israelites' for that matter was like in those days? Every time a warrior threw his head backwards the head covering opened to reveal the formerly obscured furrows and fearsome forehead of a warrior. Many warriors in the day and age of David used this tactic to intimidate their opponents by the sheer ugliness and ostensibly fearless faces (especially the furrowed browses).

When Goliath thought of throwing his head back wards to expose his hideous forehead as a tactic, David saw an opportunity and shot right in the middle of the then furrowed browse. Goliath was dead just because David knew the reality of spotting an opportunity. God gave him that ability and he employed it. Whilst our Lord Jesus Christ is our guide, I only used David since he represents in this instance a person thought lowly of. His own father forgot about him when the prophet Samuel came in search of the one to be king. Samuel himself thought one of his brothers was the one instead of David. His own father made him heard sheep alone in the thickets of the bushes. His brothers made jokes of him and thought of him mad and a show off when he dared confront Goliath.

David knew that what he possessed was far more than any man could convince him otherwise. He was made fun of, ridiculed and thought of as mad but it did not deter him from pursuing his goal and from putting to public use what God had put in him during his days as a shepherd. He was well aware of God's calling in his life and he was ready to follow it. He never at the time try to run away from it as sufferers sometimes do when we meet our present day Goliath. We should all know our call and stay within its boundaries. David knew his call: the call to kill Goliath and this pagan Goliath knew his call: the call to die miserably! Oh My!

PROPELLED BY A VISION TO GET A BREAKTHROUGH

Without a vision the hope of a breakthrough deaden in the seemingly engaged lines of a silent heaven and creates a Riga mortis on a live hope. David's ability and charisma to view the mascular frame of Goliath trampling down, his head cut off his neck and his flesh fed to the vultures of the air way before it all happened threw him nearer to the reality of getting a victory. The other seldom pulpit favourites are the hopes of what he was to be granted by undertaking this exploit; David was promised years of non taxation, a princess for a wife and many other perks. These among other things got him fired up for the work. He burned with a passion to show the Philistine of his time that his God was greater than any six or null legged pagan god and any of the gods of this world for that matter.

Among all the seven hundred expect stone throwers who could (as the Bible proclaims) shoot a stone at a hair's breath, a young man with an eye to see the unseen, visualise the future and adored God went forth with the battle. The others wetted their armours at the site of Goliath. They had no vision of what the future held, only a haze of what the present Philistine studded battlefield their bodies reposed on shone through their tear flooded eyebrows.

Without a burning passion for a vision, life looks like a layman's history for a lost cause. Light a fire inside your spirit, burn ablaze with a passion to surmount your mountains whatever they are. A visionary man cannot be stopped. He will cry out "...son of David have mercy on me..." even if they tell him to shut up. A desperate person will tear off a roof and come to Jesus for his healing. There is always a pressing in and a never quitting tendency with the hearts of those who are visionary.

You have to get hungry and desperately thirsty if you are expecting a breakthrough.

"If you draw nigh to God and He will draw nigh to you"

You have to make a move first, that is a principle. Get the sap of the Holy Spirit to rise within the depth of your inner being and move towards God. He did his part when he first loved you before you even knew him, but now it's your time to hunger for a breakthrough. Be thirsty, the time is coming for a breakthrough what can you lack when you have a God who says He is El-shaddai- the Lord who is more than enough? What can you not perceive when you have a God who proclaims He is Jehovah Jireh-the Lord who sees to it and if He sees to it then He can provide?

How can you not have a vision for your healing when God says He is Jehovah Rapha- the Lord that healeth thee? What deliverance do you miss when you have a God who says He is Jehovah Nissi-Yahweh is my banner? Who can be against you when your God proclaims He is Jehovah Shamma- the Lord is there?

Push forward; get hungry for your vision. When you take hold of it, keep talking about it, keep saying it, keep thinking about it, have a sort of spiritual soliloquy as it were for the word of God says He is able,

"...to give more abundantly than we can ever ask or *think*..."

A PARADIGM SHIFT OBSERVED

The scriptures are never on a faux-pass level, you have to think about it every step of the way. It might seem a foolish principle an author desperate to soothe fists of pain picked up and pocketed but if you can perceive a breakthrough within you then you can overcome but if you can not you are not fulfilling Scripture for the word again concurs,

"...for as a man thinketh so is he..."

If you fulfil without changing your mindset then rest assured God only did it as an act of benevolence (charity). You are called not to bailing out, crying out, crying aloud but to sticking it out so have a clear paradigm shift and deny to survive In a survival mode.

Revamp your thinking pattern, if you are to aim for the highest mark you will always surmount and without fail leave behind the moiety of your previous self.

A sufferer's main problem is verbalising self fulfilling prophesies. The scripture in proverbs says "we are snared by the words of our mouth" if we in our predicament utter negative words we will get negative results for we will always reap what we sow. If we say we cannot then nothing will come up. If we say we don't think we might surmount then we will only get what we say. We can not talk defeat and expect to live in victory. Human nature always wants to talk about the problem more than the how to get out of it issues. It is better to say nothing than to say negative things which will surely self fulfil.

Zacharius' negative words made God allow dumbness to come upon him. Mephibosheth's own words and mentality made him to stay in mediocrity for more than half of his life. David's own words made God to recognise him as a man after His own heart. You have to take note that your circumstances obey the words of your mouth. Your tongue has the ability to turn your sadness into happiness and your nights into morning. It also has the ability to sit you comfortable in your pain and suffering.

No matter how it looks child of God sow seed of good words and before you know it, a breakthrough will surely arrive due to the power of positive words. Practise it in your life everyday for there are no guarantees that pain and suffering will surely be done away with in this life (note I am saying in this life). To everything there is a reason and a season and since I am an author analysing one of the biggest problems on earth I will not feed my audience with a nonexistent certainty that pain is going to seize in this present world (With the exclusion when Christ comes), no that I will not do.

But if there be seasons in this world we live in, that means these seasons will be at the magnitude of biblical proportions; "To everything there is a season, and a time to every purpose under the heavens: A time to be born and a time to die; A time to kill and a time to heal; A time to break down and a time to build up; A time to weep and a time to laugh; A time to mourn and a time to dance...A time for war and a time for peace" If this becomes the order of the seasons then I am in my sound mind as a message bearer to call for a practise of this paradigm shift everyday of our lives so as to be able to adapt to these changing seasons. We should all be able to speak positive words into our situations for our words are more often than not, self-fulfilling.

Prophesy then, to the magnitude of your suffering and your pain. David prophesied to the Goliath of his day and told him about his God. He did not tell God about his problem for God knew his obstacle but rather, he got his problem acquainted with the magnitude of his God. That is a clear mindset and a divine vision. A great paradigm shift.

There are no engaged lines to heaven. God hears when you prophesy to the dry bones and the Goliath of your life. He is not a pot bellied Buda who can possess seven hands which are too short to deliver. He is not Allah who gives commission to kill innocent people with no sign of remorse. Ronald Dunn gave the following analogy on the reality of God always answering prayers that are biblically sound and buried in his will. Ronald Dunn's story goes:

"God sent me some light in a surprising way. We were in Arkansas visiting my brother and his family, and the county fair was in full swing. One night we loaded everybody into the car and went to the fair. We were not there long before it became obvious that our children were not interested in the blue-ribbon hogs or the award winning heifers. They wanted to get to the rides. So, abandoning the more cultural aspects of the fair, we headed for the carnival and candyfloss.

All the rides were 10 cents apiece. We bought a big roll of red 10-cent tickets and got organised. At the time my brother had one child, Rebecca; I had three-Ron, Jr., Steven and Kimberly. I positioned myself at the entrance of the rides and as the kids came by, holding out their hands, I tore off a red 10-cent ticket and gave it to them.

I was standing at the entrance to the Tilt-A-Whirl with the roll of tickets. First, Rebecca came by, holding out her hand, and I gave her a ticket. Then Kimberly came by with her hand out and I gave her a ticket. Ronnie was next, then Steven, each holding out his hand for a red 10-cent ticket.

Right behind Stephen came a little boy I had never seen in my life – holding out his hand for a red 10-cent ticket. Who is this kid? What is he trying to pull? These tickets cost 10 cents apiece – you do not go around giving them away to every kid who has his hand out. The boy stood there, hand outstretched, waiting. I ignored him. He stood there; the line behind him began to pile up. Would-be Tilt-A-Whirl riders grew restless and demanded to know what the hold up was. Finally, Stephen turned around, pointed to this importunate little beggar and said, 'Dad, this is my friend. I told him you would give him a ticket.'

Friend! We had not been there twenty minutes. I looked down. The boy was still standing there, holding out his hand.

Do you know what I did? I tore off a red 10-cent ticket and gave him – not because I wanted to, or because he deserved it, but because my son had told this boy that his dad would give him a ticket. I was not about to embarrass my son or make him out to be a liar.

Tough he did not realize it, the little boy was asking for a ticket 'in Steven's name'. And I gave him a ticket 'in Steven's name'. I made good the word of my son.

Then I saw it. That is it! I go to the father and say, 'Your son said that if I ask for a red 10-cent ticket, you will give me one.' I ask in Jesus' name and the Father gives in Jesus' name.

The father makes good the word of his son."

I as an author have not yet found a better explanation from a fellow author (The ones whose material I have been blessed to read that is) on God's modes operandi to answer your prayers more than the revelation God gave Ronald Dunn. It should be noted however that we all need to be in the will of God and also have applied every ingredient God requires of us to have in order to get a breakthrough. God is faithful, He says my word will not return to me void but it will accomplish its assigned undertaking. I do not need any more assurances than this to know God will never leave me without being shepherded. I am all for God's promises for this world holds nothing close to what God has so through my pain and my seemingly unending suffering I shall wait upon His word to accomplish that which He has assigned it to accomplish and before I know it, there it is, my breakthrough.

THE MENU OF A BREAKTHROUGH

Tantamount a menu there needs to be a lucid balance in the ingredients. Getting off the fragile edges of anguish is no difference; it requires a sufferer to balance all the requirements to be applied.

In the Valley of Dry Bones Ezekiel receives a word to prophecy to the dry bones after he first had a burning desire to speak to God. Within half of no time God tells him to speak to the dry bones and make flesh come to them. Flesh really came on them but still the breath had not and God had to tell him to prophecy to the breath.

If Ezekiel had ended at the flesh coming to the bones then the miracle would simply have been incomplete, it is as simple to understand as that. In your predicament God expects you to follow every step, one step at a time for him to give you a breakthrough. A sinner can not quote the scripture that says 'everything will work together for those who love God' and expect things to work together, it is impossible because that same scripture proclaims you have to love God first so as to have everything to work together and loving God is seen by obeying the words of those He sent.

YOUR PROBLEM WILL BOW TO GOD

The Bible says Goliath fell face down after the sling shot hit him on the forehead. It is scientifically senseless to fall face down after having been engulfed by a pain that is forcefully going back wards and in all power causing someone as large as Goliath to die. Close analysis shows that when God gives you a breakthrough it tears to pieces, shreds and burns to smoke all points of reason. By Goliath falling face down, Goliath in his entire blasphemous mouth acknowledged the power of the sovereign God.

There is a word for you, no matter how big your Goliath is, God is able and willing to make that problem bow to Him.

CHAPTER ELEVEN

SOMETHING IS ABOUT TO HAPPEN

Silence like a poultice, most of the time comes from the fathomless depths to soothe the dabs of notes. In proverbial philosophy well timed silence has more eloquence than speech. It is in itself that seemingly soporific mother of indigence for prayer that makes faith become the midwife; it commences with one's heart, spills into the soul, and unfolds with impending emotion until it is rewarded through faith, by grace. Silence propels our inner most beings to react with hope of many unseen better morrows.

"Weeping may endure for a night but joy cometh in the morning" [Psalms 30 vs. 5]

When God is silent the miraculous might behind that tense atmosphere a sufferer experiences, distils a believer's complexity into one explosive breakthrough that dissolves the acute episodes of that perdition. By handling pain as a temporary circumstance mingled in permanent circumstances the Psalmist aids us to experience

God in a reinvigorated dimension so as to seize the moment and terminate the ravaging storms of our lives. Come what may, God remains loving, inerrant and sufficient. He remains the same God who plants His footsteps in the raging oceans and rides the storm. To say He is a God of love will be a clear understatement for God is love. Love bears all things, endures all things. He will never forsake you.

THE COUNCIL OF FOOLS

God's affability and sotto-voce blesses even in the midst of your storms. Bear in mind that your destiny is seldom bound to those who walk away and that experiencing unnatural grace comes only by fellowshipping with the mystery of God. It is the only camaraderie that transcends everything seen or unseen, race or colour.

More often than not humanity's catastrophes are birthed from ill company, craving for reckless haste, ill founded ambitions and misdirected visions but God loves us still. He endows us with divine gifts to better understand our purpose and destiny, but common sense has become less common to our human mind in this day and age that we have forfeited the intellect of our superintendence and Bata-traded if for malicious malady.

Our minds got engraved by Hades' silversmiths, we see no better than we stumble, we set off for one destination but stumble into another ring road with no hope of acquiring an antidote out of the mess yet God employs pain to retain us in to our ordained destiny. It will still be silence, still graphic, it might be still suffering but how we surmount it ushers glory to the author of our life and faith.

HOODWINKED

Many of the times like in Christian Heraclites, we are so hoodwinked to our mortal entanglements that we dare not to call upon God, dreading He would decamp us from our cravings. This is the time we experience grief in the taste of silence yet at the swallow of it, arrives the satisfaction stationed in the wake of a breakthrough. If we are to walk with a mystery and experience a mystery then we should consider pain and work on demolishing our idleness God's way, for idleness is only the holiday of nincompoops.

There is need always to analyse our prayer alters and rebuild them before we jump to confusions and conclude that our suffering is God authored. Sometimes our suffering commences from absconding the presence of God, which might have caused us to miss what God had to say in our lives. Even so, we are called to resist the devil and at the same time be victorious and happy when he attacks for it just proves how God values us as his children.

If it hurts the devil so much that you are in God's presence then the battle is even more interesting for you than it is for the devil. After all what is localised pain compared to the joyful floods of eternity?

WHAT IF I...

> "But he (Stephen) full of the Holy Ghost... said, behold I see the heavens opened and the son of man standing on the right hand of the God ...they (accusers) cried out... and stoned Steven... [Acts 7 vs. 55-58]

If in the midst of God's silence you surmount but fail to find utter solace (it does not happen if you obey God anyway) and you are drawn from the quiver, shot into the dart board of opportunity at least you can shout "I have had the chance to examine the extent of my destiny", then wait upon the rhema of God. Bear in mind however that God's silence is always his sotto-voce and in it rests the power that broke Peter's jail chains, tore the curtains of the temple, darkened the skies, and divided the masses of water. There is also success in failure because failure is in itself a sign that if you can see your failure then at least you have a testimony that you are surviving. In a nutshell, a step discarded is another step forward.

Stephen experienced it and in his account lays the extraordinary power that moves among ordinary men so as to demolish the chains of serfdom. He was content with suffering even unto death. Death awaited him but he never aborted it in prayer, instead he prayed for God to forgive those who stoned him. Unlike Job, Stephen had seen the unsung verses of his life hanging in the brightness of heaven.

Note: in my Bible this is the only verse Jesus is seen just standing in Heaven. There was silence on earth yet in heaven Christ was "standing" Oh my!

Pray with me: oh Lord, Heavenly Father hallowed IS thy name. In mine pain and suffering stand beside the "Stephen" of my heart. Adorn me with Heavenly wonder, that shining armour so that in the shadow of death when life to me seems near an end; shall your love flow to the depth of mine heart and even if I die before I wake, I pray, my soul do keep. When death looms nigh to me let me be able to shout like Paul that to live is Christ and to die is gain. In Christ's holy name. AMEN.

WHO CAN UNDERSTAND GOD?

"...who hath known the mind of the Lord...
But we have the mind of Christ [1 Corinthians 2vs. 16]

Coincidence is God's pseudonym when He prefers to remain anonymous. Neither man is an entire island on itself nor an accident at its peak. We are all endowed with a divine purpose and even more, with the ability to know the mind of God through the mind of Christ. Too pregnant a statement but wholly divine.

Apostle Paul's epistle to the Corinthians explores the believer's God given complexity that sets them apart from sinners- the ability to understand the mind of our Creator. Not acknowledging him opens and propels us into a tract of darkness and obscurity where those who dwell, dwell alone. It is in this malevolent vacuum that the devil rides high into the level of our own mortal entanglements, forces us into tying ourselves to them, thereby forfeiting our God given ability to subdue the earth God's way through the Holy Spirit.

THE FELLOWSHIP AND THE PAIN

The greatest fellowship is that of the Holy Spirit. "Parakletos" which means in Greek both to speak to and speak for you. With this camaraderie in one's life comes the understanding of God's will: nothing, absolutely nothing will ever succeed against a believer. With this person in us we will be able to say to a mountain in our life move and it moves, crumble and it crumbles. This is true faith to which the Bible says "...have the faith of God" and also says "...let this mind be in you that was also in Jesus..."

We need to have an unadulterated understanding of how to receive from God and to live in the fullness of the life God filled us with through Christ. I am here going to quote Sigmund Freud (as if he has a lot to say), but where he says a sensible thing I am inclined by my own understanding to capitalise on it. Sigmund says every average human being has at least three dreams per night. The biblical Mr Job concurs "For God speaketh once, yea twice, yet man perceive it not. In a dream, in a vision when deep sleep falls upon man in slumberings upon a bed..." This shows that God is always speaking to men in dreams and visions through the person of the Holy Spirit on other cases but men fail to hear him so we have to try and understand God's way of talking for and to us so as to surmount the great evil of pain. We all can hear God and understand him according to what scripture says and by it we possess the mind of God as Paul put it. It is the Apostle Paul who said it and not me.

Since we have the mind of the author of our life and faith, let us therefore walk in the light of His word- logos and the fulfilment of the rhema-God's saying word so as to fulfil our call, that call to be vessels of honour ready for the master's use. The battle has already been won, what is left for us to do now is to walk in the ring and claim the victory. The path has been discovered in Christ even in that silence what is left is to just walk it.

When you feel you are perishing remember we are all fighting a fixed fight. In Jesus we have everything to gain, neither devil nor time can impede us, before and through Christ's death and resurrection we like Him have "…overcome the world…" Remember victory is born out of a struggle. Nothing just happens unless God permits it. Even the devil has to ask permission to mess up with your life [Job 1 vs. 12]

Rebuild your alters even in the midst of suffering. Come boldly before the throne of grace and find mercy. It is one thing to believe in His word and another to understand His mind. BUT WE HAVE THE MIND OF CHRIST and the last time I checked, the steps of the righteous are still ordered by the Lord and if Christ surmounted and I having His mind as Apostle Paul says can overcome also…

DON'T HATE THE COACH, HATE THE GAME
if you will.

God created everything in its right state. In fact God after finishing creation says "…good…" Evil is not created; it is neither a thing nor a creature that it may be created but simply a *privation*. With this in mind take note that God being a creator of everything could not have created some*thing* that is not a thing. Evil came as a result of the fall of men and the continual demonic choices of men so for God to stop it there needs to be in Him a need to destroy the cause of the problem of evil and that cause is us, the human beings.

The ability to choose will be terminated also if God is to uproot every corner where evil lies hiding. Where there is power to choose you get all sorts of choices, bad or right, evil or righteous. God is not a remote control and humans are not a cosmic joke driven by the former. If this world still exists and we the causes of evil still exist then there will always be pain and suffering and God might employ this pain at his own discretion with the intention of moving us into the path of our destiny. He employs and not creates it for the reason mentioned in Hebrews vs. 10 " This happened that we might not rely on ourselves but on God" But good news to those who believe in God for Christ says "Be of good cheer for I have overcome the world."

Do not contemplate death or taking your life as many have because that will make the above statement a lie when God Himself can not lie. Note the Bible in the letter of Apostle Paul to Titus does not say God does not lie, it says God *can not lie*.

IT IS MY LIFE ANYWAY!

Dear world, I am leaving you because I am bored, I am leaving you with your worries. Good luck. (Sanders George – suicide note)

How then can we understand God whilst drowning in pain? Is it with dribbling saliva of a dunderhead or with the spirit within? If we can neither understand Him nor perceive His will for our suffering will we be justified to implode and end our austere and rotten lives, gaze towards another in the golden streets of the world unseen by this present eye?

The equations and poetries of all our lives are never solved by ending our own lives. This method of trying to escape the realities and pain in this world is nothing more than a quick and horrible path to another world of immense pain. God takes suicide just as he does, murder. He takes it as if the one who committed suicide has killed someone (revelation) - and that someone will be you the committer of that suicide.

It is understandable to feel sorry for those (including me) who have lost relatives and loved ones through this evil but committing suicide is a latent avalanche of misconception (I say this with love and with a great understanding that there is a possibility that the one who commits suicide might repent after harming themselves but before dying). In fact suicide is a sure sign of defeat and rebellion to the word of God because it exhibits evidence that you could not rise above your situation when God said:

> "You can not be tempted above that which you can not overcome…"

Why make God a liar by just a failure to adhere to His word? There is absolutely no pain you can not quench by the word of God if you abide in the shelter of the Almighty. No evil you can not surmount if God says He knows it then you have a sure word and going against is rebelling against God who said it. It should be noted with a great mind that life is not always a 'keyboard, Dilbert principle' where we keep our eyes and set our fingers on the escape button. Sometimes we just have to unreservedly fight it out.

The real problem we face in this world is that of plagiarism, we have used Christ's words without informing our hearers on the power of the *Source* who said them. The world as a result has become a diabolic pool surviving on comparing morals and principles. There is to the world no lucid difference between the authority of Christ and that of the schizophrenic Hitler. The world through secular humanism has ignored the importance of Authority behind the words yet it is that seemingly foolish and antiquated principle of teaching the morals by quoting the author of the morals that redeems.

Someone said "In periods of unsettled faith, scepticism, and mere curious speculation in matters of religion, teachers of all kinds swarm like the flies in Egypt. The demand creates the supply. The hearers invite and shape their own preachers. If the people desire a calf to worship, a ministerial calf-maker is readily found." Paul said, "I proclaimed to you the testimony of God." I, like him will neither want to tinkle the ears of my audience with what they want to hear if it is not divinely accurate, nor awash their senses with empty truisms obtained from renegade or good authors who are deficient in inspiration. By so saying I am geared at providing what truth only dictates be it, it is painful or sorrowful and I will always inform my audience of the Authority behind the words.

To deprive humanity of the above is tantamount regarding our lord Jesus Christ as a mere moral teacher when He is more than that. C.S Lewis said of Christ and I agree "A man who was merely a man and said the sort of things Jesus said would not be a great moral teacher. He would either be a lunatic-on the level with a man who says he's a poached egg-or else he'd be the devil of hell. You must make your choice. Either this man was, and is, the Son of God, or else a madman or something worse" With this mind set we are blessed by a sure word that whatever Christ says is a word to be trusted beyond depth and beyond height. If He says we are never going to be tested beyond that which we can overcome then there is no reason for demising since we have a breakthrough staring us in the face.

Anyway what is in suicide that you, your loved ones or I need to give it a chance instead of surmounting our suffering through God's word? Dorothy Parker wrote of the vanity of suicide:

> **Razors pain you:**
> **Rivers are damp;**
> **Acids stain you;**
> **And drugs cause cramp.**
> **Guns are not lawful;**
> **Nooses give;**
> **Gas smells awful;**
> **You might as well live.**

Life is so precious to live than spend it contemplating death; this will be a gross error. The fact that you are alive though thinking of demising is a sure sign that you have a reason to rejoice for you are still breathing. In a sense you have survived, and that on its own is a breakthrough. Let us not transform God from a creator to a duplicator by envying those who are seldom suffering, those surmounting or those long gone.

It is those same people who do lack visions or expectation who suffer little because they lack expectations but if you expect the greatest out of life, pain then becomes the key to greater exploits. Rejoice for God has given you a key and all you need to accomplish is finding the door to your destiny and this is not an inflexible thing to bring about because our lord Jesus Christ said 'I am the door.' He neither said He was one of the doors nor did He say He might be the door. You have a true and definite word that He is the door and if you have the key surely you can enter. Take it in your spirit that even if you are in pain, pain does not have you. If you have suffering, suffering does not own you. You are of God and your tears are just but a touch of reality and a prayer the devil can not and will not impede.

God is not a son of man that He may lie. There is a time coming, you might not know when but do not conceive a mentality of ending it all. It is not worth it. You are more than a conqueror. There are two levels to the perception of the grandeur and the horror of suicide. The first is to think of suicide in the same level with Nietzsche's lies in Beyond good and Evil which says that the 'thought of suicide is a great comfort: It is a good way of getting through many a bad night' and the other which is a little sensible from the mouth of Greer which proclaims in the Observer Review that 'suicide is an act of narcissistic manipulation and deep hostility.' The reality is all these contributions might be considered obliging by some people yet there is a need to take a big deep breathe and proclaim that Christ is our exemplar not Nietsche or any other crazy or supposed thinker out there.

Hear is the very truth we seek, if God as a spirit is not committing suicide, bolting out, exploding or miserable due to the moral decadence and the vast cultural derelict in this world then you being born of this same Spirit can overcome every obstacle strewn in your highways and byways. Remember you are a spirit having a mere natural experience and it is in the natural that pain is and not in the spiritual. You and I should as believers endeavour to live in the spiritual everyday so as to evade the clutches of pain in the natural.

Just believe you have overcome, do not hope you will come out of your situation but believe you have for the word 'hope' without substance is by definition 'doubt postponed' Have faith, the 'now' faith. The word of God says 'Now faith is…' It does not say 'now faith will be', it does not say 'now faith hopes it shall or was' but it says 'Now faith is…' receive what you pray for in your spirit, believe your predicament has already been terminated. That is to have the faith of God as the Bible rightly calls it. When you have it, the Spirit of God will bear testimony with your spirit that you are an over comer and not a failure.

God's word never fails, godly patience will never be impatient, godly temperance never tires, godly will never wishes, godly must is never a might'. You are an over comer in Christ for His yes is never a 'maybe' or a 'was' that you may hide your head within the sand like an ostrich.

In all your embankment into the path of overcoming your pain if you feel like you are failing never lose heart. Failing is different from failure; failure only comes after someone quits. Failing is success trying to be born, so move up the pace, grow so ever hungry for a breakthrough, examine your altars and move on until it comes for it shall surely come. Surround yourself with positive believers who can motivate you, help you load all the negative views in to the refuse tank and prepare to be blessed.

No one can ever feel the pain of the afflicted, it is impossible to do that. It is also useless and unreasonable to utter the words "I know how you feel" because it is hard to feel someone's pain so do not look for people you feel will; understand your pain at the same level with you. Only God and the sufferer can understand the degree of pain experienced and if we as believers overpower this evil among us then let us take the lessons learnt during these times of trials to enrich and comfort those who might be contemplating the worst or those who might be simply passing through a hard patch in life, after all pain though dreadful is simply a gift. The truth is evident that in all our pain and suffering we are all fighting a fixed fight anyway.

A FIXED FIGHT

Patience is a virtue and it only comes to those who wait. I agree with Ronn Dunn that the fight between Jacob and the angel was a fixed fight, for no one can fight God's angel and win. It had to be fixed. Not only does the angel fight Jacob he even pulls a fit of a miracle by injuring him right on the hip just by a mere touch but Jacob holds on to him. What surprises me most about Jacob's character is even when his hip could not carry him, he kept holding to that even the angel had to complain about the length of the fight.

"...look the morning is nigh..."

Jacob kept on keeping on. Many a time we lose the fight because we let go of the hunger to win too soon. Surmounting the calamities in our lives requires a God inhabitant heart that keeps on fighting even when parts of our beings are no longer operational. There is tremendous power in Jesus to get us to surmount this rollercoaster of suffering. I wish I could describe this Jesus to you:

THIS JESUS

Has nothing in his being called a real world for He knows no distinction between the physical and the spiritual realms.

My Jesus speaks to trees and they wither, He speaks and commands a corpse to rise from its slumber and it comes back to life. He curses diseases and they seize, demons tremble at His name. He never held a funeral procession. When He died the dead rose from the dead. When He rose they paraded themselves alive in the cities. He sits at the centre of the universe; He is the chief executive officer of the universe. The words from His mouth are life. At His word mountains move and devils flee. He is as real today as He was when He walked on the streets of Jerusalem. In Him there is no sin and there is absolutely no shadow of turning.

I do not know if you really believe in Him or *know* him but if you dare to believe He will move your pain for you and tread your suffering under your feet. We have to have a profound tenacity to capsize the vicissitudes of life and stare at them lying vulnerable under our God given authority. You are already endowed by that certain favour that when you begin to know the intensity of it you will burn with the fire of a breakthrough. Words alone can not fully describe this Jesus.

USING YOUR FAVOUR TO GET A BREAKTHROUGH

Use your favour against your calamity. Do not wish to use it or want to, for wanting is just the same as wishing. You will never go anywhere with a wish. Tell your innermost being that you are going to use your favour. When you say you are going to use it, that's called a decision and a decision is above wishes and wants.

Favour is a catalyst that quickens and changes substantiated hope into reality. By the time you start using favour against your famine people will start noticing, let alone talking. Many will esteem you, rejoice in your height but never forget that the same people who Hosanna you today will shout "crucify" him the next.

If you can smile in the middle of a storm then your favour will not remain dormant. Get yourself ready to activate your breakthrough through enacting your favour. Wisdom is the ability to use knowledge concerning the potency of your favour. It is a pole vaulting stance to leap in to heights that will propel us to the upper wheels of life. Above all let us be extremely vigilant in comprehending the value of pain in our lives and the reality of our intimacy with the creator, and Saviour Jesus Christ.

Ultimately I do not wish to leave the reader with a mind that says God can never be silent because He can be. The book of Samuel says it in a more revelatory manner "…in those days the word of the Lord was rare; there were not many visions…" By so saying it should be noted that God does not become silent for the fun of it otherwise I like H.G wells will justifiably shout "If I thought there was a God who looked down on battles and death and all the waste and horror of this world- able to prevent these things - *doing them to amuse Himself*, I would spit in His empty face" BUT God the Almighty one does not employ pain (at the time He employs it) to amuse himself but does it for our unadulterated benefit. He does not even cause pain.

With the realisation of favour a sufferer can get lost in the spirit and power to surmount that they will without fail take notice of their present situation, opium if you like but a good one. It is a comprehensible loss to miss the point that favour is above any predicament the devil throws at us. Suffering may come in divers ways but it has no power over a sufferer who understands the value and impact of their favour in Christ. It is that simple but we have to realise and apprehend the reality of this favour in our agonizing lives.

It is said there are two kinds of people among both the sane, the absolutely crazy and the semi-crazy – There are those that wake up every other morning and say, "Good morning Lord", ready to use their favour for their advantage and there are those among the mad and the semi-mad who wake up every morning, fail to realise their favour and instead of saying "Good morning Lord" they say, "Lord, it is morning". They are ready to demise because the man in them is far weak and far rotten that understanding the power within them and the favour endowed in them is a pleasure too expensive to be explored.

PAIN, MAN AND GOD

It is of great importance to understand that sometimes being human complicates our mindset and unless the author of our life places a fire under us we will never move. These burning charcoals motivate and force us to alter and change our lives usually for the better. Pain, anguish, suffering all in all and through and through correct and perfect the man in us. Pain is in itself a tool to inspect, direct and at times protection in that pain can prevent you from pursuing the worst in life. Pain may come to you in the form of an unanswered prayer but before you complain take note of what Mr Graham's wife was quoted as having said "If all my prayers were answered then I would have married the wrong person, seven times"

This gospel of pain has for long been omitted both in theological circles and on ministry level, yet it is something the church should not go without even if it could and couldn't do without even if it should. We also have forgotten it in our own families; we have taught our kids, friends and families subjects ranging from salvation to escatology but forgot to tell them what made us tick, PAIN.

THE STORM IS OVER

Jeremiah has a well of hope within him. He has been prophesying about a siege coming to Jerusalem and there was a possibility of everyone taken as captives yet he buys land from Hanamel. Though he can simply be send to exile because of all his tautology one thing remains in him that God's promise of Israel forever being owned by Israel as a nation, shall forever stand. That is an unadulterated trust in a covenanting God.

The word of God is full of facts and no possibilities. God says if you abide within my shelter a thousand may fall at your..., He says pain may endure for a night but blessing cometh...He says I will never forsake you nor...Those are all facts they do not need connotations yet it requires a mind with a Jeremiah spirit of buying where others are selling in the anticipation of a gloom future. The storm is over! Take it in to your spirit. It is over! Your pain is over!

BEFORE THE END OF THE STORM

Instead of trying to push God into making us happy with all the answers to our prayers I wish to unmask the paradox: leading every human, suffering, pained or not to a level where we make God happy instead. We as humans always like to exhibit a theological stand of a God that blesses without getting to grips with the God that punishes and a God that hides his face when sin engulfs our lives and also a God that employs pain as an agent for greater divine exploits. Though we like to sing 'have your way lord in our lives…' we have changed into borrowed robes of analysers of God rather than analysers of our lives and ourselves with regards to who God wants us to be.

Our goals can never be altered until we put forth a willingness to renew our minds, manage and comprehend a God that enjoys a simple smile from His creation in the midst of trials. We have become a people striving through a survival mode. We have managed to throw away the reality of living life and exercising faith in a dry place swamped by risks, pain, anguish and twinge. Suffering has become to us simply a punishment from what seems to us an inconsiderate God, hence we forget that pain and suffering are just but valuable pieces of the gospel that the church forgot and treasures and nuggets of riches the body of Christ wants to escape. To introduce pain as a vehicle God uses to sharpen us for greater exploits and as an abnormal normality to this world will be running against the grain with this present church.

We are in this world operating in an absurdity called "circular humanism". The truth itself is masked and referred to as rigid and oft as not being open minded but when I sharpen my pencils and clip my biros I still have a revelation that though I am not an entire Island on itself there are people who do not believe in the sensibleness of pain and because of this they thrive on hope without substance. Instead of hoping to surmount, they should surmount! But hope without substance is simply **"DOUBT POSTPONED"** Partial disobedience is disobedience, delayed obedience is disobedience and waving faith is faith contaminated. Get it in your mind that it is seldom for a person to get in life anymore than they put in and at the time they put in because a person's harvest is mainly determined by the time, amount, type and value of seeds he sows.

However, the mere fact that you have read the previous chapters of this book is a clear sign that you are not comfortable within your suffering and within the chains of the predicament you are experiencing. By this mere fact your inner being is showing you that if you can not fit in the predicament then the life you have been living is far beyond what God intends you live in. God is ready to give you a breakthrough that is why he says:

"After you have suffered a while…"

The whole answer to the problem of pain lies in the chapter's unseen and unread by our natural eye and the mindset a sufferer shields within their heart. In these lie the will of God for our suffering and the will of God will never take us where the grace of God will not be sufficient enough to keep us. "After you have suffered a while…" as a statement shows that there is a reason behind the suffering experienced. What is this present pain anyway that we may lose eternity due to our grumbling? only chuff, a shadow on the run, to be exact and a thing to be surmounted, to be truthful. C.S Lewis says "Pain insists upon being attended to. God whispers to us in our pleasures, speaks to us in our conscience and shouts to us in our pain. It is His megaphone to rouse a deaf world"

What the devil meant for conflict, God meant for conquer. What he meant for death God meant for life. What he meant for pain God meant for good. Reader, it is not worth walking in pain without a desire to revamp the system of pain's serfdom of us. It is not possible to obtain a victory without a war being fought and many a sweet victory comes from many a frightening fight or many a painful encounters.

We have to press towards our goal and not lose hope; you and I are *too blessed to be stressed*.

We have to tell our adversary that we may be still in the projects but we are ready to move up. We might be in prison but we are ready to be acquitted. We might be in the ruins of Nagasaki but we are about to move up. We might be in the bushes of Djibouti Africa yet shall we rise from our ashes. We might be in the derelict streets of Peru or Asia yet shall the power in us cause us to rise. We might simply be in stress, suffering and in pain yet in the flamboyant streets of America, Britain or Europe but God is ready to get us out. It is the beauty of grace, something religion can not give us. With it we are endowed by a force far bigger than our circumstance.

Though we look as if in chains, the power within the word is not bound. It is this same power that mounts us with wings of eagles and causes us to run and never get weary. It is this power to triumph that gives us courage to call the things that are not as if they were. That system can be without reservation described in one word, FAITH. In it is the power and desire to get out of our situation.

The many battles of life have been fought and won in the pages of the spiritual realm what now is left for you and I as sufferers is to bring without fail these victories in to the physical realm were they can be viewed and read. Their manifestation into the physical realm rests on us, the burden of proof lies on us. We have to take hold of the truth that victory has been obtained and what is left is a need for a people who understand the principles of this present life to get in to a position where they can receive this victory. Let us not be dog like stooges.

We have to get tired and ashamed of chewing yesterday's vomits. Be able to move within the move of God, desire the best out of life and strive to obtain a quantum leap and enlarge our capacity to embody a breakthrough. Sometimes life can be too short to be spent mourning over spilt milk. Every time we get in a catastrophic moment let us get it into our brains that we are too blessed to be stressed. *We are too sacred to be sorry, too sanctified to be sacked, too great to be small and most importantly too hallowed to suffer* more than that which is necessary. We are all *sentenced to blessing*; we can not run away from this truth even if wanted to.

It is not what God is doing *to* you, but what God is doing *for* you.

THE WEAVER

The great preacher said "my life is but a weaving between my lord and me; I can not choose the colours he worketh steadily. If He weaveth sorrow and I in foolish pride forget he sees the upper and I the underside. The dark threads are as needful in the weaver's skilful hand as the threads of gold and silver in the pattern he has planned. Not till the loom is silent and the shuttle cease to fly shall God unroll the canvas and explain the reason why."

This great analogy is strengthened by Francis I Anderson when he says, 'Men seek an explanation of suffering in cause and effect. They look backward for a connection between prior sin and present suffering. The Bible looks forward in hope and seeks explanations, not so much in origins as in goals. The purpose of suffering is seen, not in its cause, but in its results. The man [in John 9:3] was born blind so that the works of God could be displayed in him"

It is therefore our duty as sufferers to understand that though we are a kind of 'supermen' in Christ we are still 'Clarks' in that sometimes we shall always suffer, for a purpose though. We are to be reminded constantly that *we are spirits having a mere natural experience*. God will always be using things that we go through in life to bring us to a destination of purity in him. There is laid for us a purpose in pain that we need to tap in to, it is God's way.

We should never get distracted by the devil on our course to maturity through pain because if we do we put up with more than that which is indispensable. We have to be able to take suffering as something we might not choose if given the dispensation to yet a valuable thing we would unquestionably not want to miss if our purpose in life was to be accomplished.

Comfort comes not only in always understanding and knowing the reasons 'why?', but in knowing the comforter who knows why?

CONFESSIONS, SCRIPTURES AND THE HIDDEN VERSES

When I first experienced a deep compelling to put these pages together I like many great writers before me went out with a thought that the most passages that bothered me most were those parts of scripture I knew nothing of or simply did not understand. But after a drooling of reasons of the 'whys' of pain I came to a point in my life both as a Christian and a Christian author where I realised that the most troubling and crippling scriptures are those I knew a lot about. Within these however came a level of understanding God's mind better than I had ever experienced. By writing to you as a Christian I also filled a gap in my own heart, answered questions that I thought unanswerable, faced truths that I never thought should be faced and above all managed to come face to face with the idea of knowing God's script of how my life will go. There in the heaven and in the Holy Scripture lies a sur ge of words containing verses and scripture about my life but:

Only God can view them and assign a measure of strength so as to let you and I carry through. God will not just be enough in our situations, He will be too much. There is a great escape in Christ that He did not come to rub it in but to rub it out so one day in the distant 'sweet by and by' if not in the 'sweet now and now' we shall all be proud of the wars we not only fought but won here on earth.

Spargeon wrote:

> 'Just as old soldiers compare stories and scars when we arrive at our heavenly home we will tell of the faithfulness of God who brought us through. I would not like to be pointed at as one who never experienced sorrow or feel like a stranger in the midst of sacred fellowship. Therefore, be content to share in the battle, for soon we will wear the crown'

Christ said we "...are the light of the world..." But in order to be what Christ says we are and be able **to provide that light we must endure burning.**

THANK YOU

To all the faceless readers who I am led to believe: have found this work to be a practical revelation within their own lives and of those around them and also to my brother Kenneth for without Him I might not have gone to God in prayer to ask Him about the problem of pain and suffering. My sincere gratitude also goes to David Yonggi Cho for the word of renewing the mind which came to me in due season, to T.D. Jakes, Kenneth Hagin Snr - God bless you, Jesse Duplantis, Pastor Chris Oyakhilome. To Hosia (Founder of Vision International Ministries) and Debrah Dzingirai for being the best of friends, the best prayer partners any sane person would wish to have and also for being our unfailing co partners in the work before us, to Oliver and wife for the exhortation, to my brother Limit Mudzanire who has without doubt seen the manifestation of God (I love you), to my brother Benjamin Mudzanire who prayed for this project and brought me to the love of Christ, Sir, I can not thank you enough. To my friend Leonard Dunira Hungwe: for being a friend and for giving your life to the Lord and to Augustine M, Sam and Purity for yielding to the call of God upon your life.

To Pastor Mike Aldaco & wife for the prophetic word (It

came to pass) and to all the New Harvest church in Manchester U.K. To Pat Robertson (700 Club) for the word of knowledge. To K.C. Price for the teaching on faith. To my In-laws Mr and Mrs Noah Madzudzo and to those to whom I have become a larger part of the only ticket in to the next generation they will ever have - my parents Mr and Mrs S.k Mudzanire and to the love of my life, my help meet, Beverly who read four scripts of this book without tiring. I am so ever blessed to have you as my wife, God bless you my love. Without fail many thanks go to Uebert Jnr for the patience. To the above and to the reader: this book unfortunately has no amplifier perhaps you could have heard me giving you a standing ovation (thanks).

To my God, Saviour, the Alpha and Omega Jesus Christ who said

> "...ye shall weep and lament...ye shall be sorrowful...In this world ye shall have trouble... John 16 vs. 20, 33] But also said "be of good cheer for I have overcome the world"

And to the Psalmist who said:

> "Many are the afflictions of the righteous but God delivers all from them"

Disclaimer

**** I testify that though my own ministry was and is still being shaped by some of the above mentioned saints of God and also by other ministries, it should be known that this book was given to me as a revelation by God Himself so it is ***not necessarily*** what the above agree or disagree with so by thanking them I do not endorse that which I have written will or can be substantiated by them. Only God can substantiate His own 'thus saith the lord' (Truth defenses itself & God fights His own wars)

REFERENCES

a) Death speaks, Jeffrey Archer, to cut the long story short (Harper Collins 2000)

b) Ronald Dunn, Don't just stand there pray something (Zondervan 1992)

c) Ravii Zacharius shuttered visage, A Challenge to atheism

d) Quotation of C.S Lewis taken from Christian reflections. Grand Rapids: Eerdmans, 1974. the problem of pain New York: The McMillan Company, 1962), Mere Christianity [New York: The Macmillan Co.,1952, pp. 40-41]

e) Dr David Yonggi Cho, Fourth dimension,(Bridge logos publishers 1979 reprinted 1999,2000,2001)

And many more important people that I listed by name within these pages: these include Spurgeon, Chinua Achebe, Bewthmore, Dorothy Parker, T.D. Jakes' Maximising the moment.

* *The Bible versions used are mainly the King James Version and the New International version unless stated

www.ingramcontent.com/pod-product-compliance
Lightning Source LLC
Chambersburg PA
CBHW031233110525
26506CB00010B/335